CREDO

An Anthology of Manifestos and Sourcebook for Creative Writing

Editors:
Rita Banerjee and Diana Norma Szokolyai

Assistant Editors:
Alexander Carrigan and Megan Jeanine Tilley

C&R Press
Conscious & Responsible

Printed in the United States of America

First Edition
1 2 3 4 5 6 7 8 9

Some of the texts featured in this anthology have appeared in print before. Acknowledgments for previous publications are listed at the end of the book.

Cover art:
The Impossibilities of My Absolute on Your Unmendable Truth by Eugenia Loli
Cover design by Laura Catherine Brown
Interior design by Ali Chica

Library of Congress Cataloging-in-Publication Data

ISBN: 978-1-936196-83-8
Library of Congress Control Number: 2018932527

C&R Press
Conscious & Responsible
crpress.org

For special discounted bulk purchases, please contact:
C&R Press sales@crpress.org
Contact info@crpress.org to book events, readings and author signings.

Suzanne Van Dam's "Writers on Location: Nature Writing Prompts" was inspired by and evolved from the teachings of Martha Gies and texts of Janet Burroway.

Nicole Walker's "On Constancy" was published in the anthology *After Montaigne*, University of Georgia Press, September 15, 2015.

Caroll Sun Yang's "Navels are Natural" was published in *The Manifest-Station*.

TABLE OF CONTENTS

CREDO

Manifestos

Craft of Writing

Exercises

CREDO

CREDO

CREDO. I believe. No other statement is so full of intent and subversion and power. A Credo is a call to arms. It is a declaration. A Credo is the act of an individual pushing back against society, against established stigmas, taboos, values, and norms. A Credo provokes. It desires change. A Credo is an artist or community challenging dogma, and putting oneself on the frontline. A Credo is art at risk. A Credo can be a marker of revolution. A Credo, is thus, the most calculating and simple form of a manifesto.

The Declaration of Independence (1776). The Communist Manifesto (1848). The Anarchist Manifesto (1850). The Symbolist Manifesto (1886). The Futurist Manifesto (1909). The Art of Noises (1913). The Dadaist Manifesto (1918). The Surrealist Manifesto (1924). The Oulipo Manifesto (1960). The Port Huron Statement (1962). The SCUM Manifesto (1967). The Cyborg Manifesto (1984). Dogma 95 (1995). Reality Hunger (2010).

CREDO (2018) is the new avant-garde. *CREDO* is our declaration against violence and limitations of free speech. *CREDO: An Anthology of Manifestos and Sourcebook for Creative Writing* is a raw look at what motivates authors today. Our *CREDO* advocates for the empowerment of female, non-binary, and marginalized literary voices, and focuses on transgender poetics, world literature and aesthetics, collage and appropriation, and the politics of place. *CREDO* is a speech act. It is a form of empowerment. *CREDO* interrogates and harkens back to political manifestos of the 19th century and modernist manifestos of the early 20th century by presenting a triad of creative writing manifestos, essays on the craft of writing, and creative writing exercises. The manifestos and craft of writing essays examine the writing process with candor and vulnerability, and the writing exercises are meant to challenge and incite creativity. In this way, *CREDO* bridges the theoretical, political, and aesthetic perspectives on contemporary writing with practical and accessible writing advice.

CREDO's ultimate mission is to highlight today's innovative writing and to provoke tomorrow's. The anthology includes pieces which reflect each writer's uncensored, unapologetic credo and what's at stake for each of our writers in each word written.

CREDO: An Anthology of Manifestos and Sourcebook for Creative Writing has been developed and edited by the Cambridge Writers' Workshop, an organization founded by Harvard alumni and based in Cambridge, MA. Our mission is to create literary programming and publications that evoke the participatory atmosphere of a literary salon, in which creative art, intellectual debate, and critical response are fostered. The Cambridge Writers' Workshop dismantles the notion that good art can only be created in either an MFA or in NYC. Rather, we aim to create a global network of creative writers, artists, and intellectuals who actively bridge their private aesthetic philosophies with their public forms of art. All writers, from novices to professionals who are looking for a serious writing community and who want to make the world vibrate just a bit, are welcome to join the Cambridge Writers' Workshop.

—Rita Banerjee
Cambridge, MA

Introduction

You wake to an alarm and clock in at work. You've got to obey the employee handbook to keep your job, talk politely and smile at people that haven't necessarily been nice to you. You have to dress a certain way. Your mother calls. Have you sent those thank you cards yet? Then, you sit through a dinner where you overhear misogynistic and racist comments coming from the other end of the table. You want to set things straight. You want to scream your truth. Then, you get home, open your writer's notebook with the unruled paper, and you are relieved that, for the first time today, your mind is meeting a platform that has no rules. You pick up your pen with the smooth, flowing ink, and you know this is your liquid voice, ready to be poured out onto the page, freely.

To write is an act of freedom. In our contemporary world, it is urgent that our voices are heard, and indeed, our creativity may be what liberates us. The act of writing empowers the individual, and it should feel thrilling. In her manifesto, "Treat Your First Draft Like a One-Night Stand," Lillian Ann Slugocki reminds us to let go of any burdens and responsibility when we write:

Treat your first draft like a one-night stand…kick your shoes across the room, play loud music, dance naked. Drink too much, and throw up on the kitchen floor. Never, ever promise to return…You are not trying to define or expand your genre. You are just having fun. You are just fucking. Again, for the sheer thrill of it. You are writing because it fucking makes you feel alive.

In the manifestos, "On Memoir" and "The Body of a Poem," we hear from the strong voices of LGBTQ+ icons Jade Sylvan and Stephanie Burt, respectively. Also from the manifestos section, David Shields declares, "I want work that, possessing as thin a membrane as possible between life and art, foregrounds the question of how the writer solves being alive. *A book should either allow us to escape existence or teach us how to endure it.*" Nell Irvin Painter inspires us and reminds us of the commitment it takes to dedicate our time to creating art.

The manifestos reveal the core of writers' identities and express the raw instincts behind the act of writing. In a fragmented, yet dogmatic world, it's important to see what people believe in. Our own beliefs are our last pillars. In an age when we don't subscribe to a unified set of social morals and values, we are rather more interested in the individual's own beliefs. This is the era of the individual. Everyone has a platform—pick your social media platform, and you will see people declaring their bite-sized credos all day long.

This anthology not only showcases the personal manifestos and credos of some of the most exciting voices on the contemporary literary scene, but it also creates a bridge from the philosophical to more practical advice for writers. In sections two and three, authors offer advice on the craft of writing and also provide writing exercises. In this way, the book's structure moves from the abstract to the concrete. Matthew Zapruder's piece "Holding a Paper Clip in the Dark" is exquisite and hopeful, as Zapruder speaks directly to the reader, with an encouraging and inviting tone: "What do I want? I want you (reader) to look at these poems as places that feel to me private to my own experience, yet also common to all of our experiences." Maya Sonenberg details very useful and insightful advice about going "Beyond the Plot Triangle." Peter Mountford humorously, but effectively writes about "Calling Bullshit on a Writer's Top 10 Excuses for Not Writing." Also in the craft of writing section, Robert Pinsky reminds us of "The Frontier of Poetry," before we have a chance to delve into the poetry of Ariel Francisco and Camille Rankine.

In the last section of the book, we are treated to a wealth of useful exercises to get the creative juices flowing. Starting with Kathleen Spivack's "The Writing Exercise: A Recipe," which illustrates the importance of setting a daily routine for writing, preferably early in the day, we also trek to advice on travel writing from Shawn Wong and benefit from nature writing prompts from Anca L. Szilágyi, S.D. Lishan, and Suzanne Van Dam. Kazim Ali closes the book with his stunning "Twelve Workshops and a Void."

This book will inspire readers to think about their own personal credos and will also serve as a functional sourcebook for creative writing advice and exercises. It is a modern scroll of raw declarations, detailing what it means to be a writer in this day and age, as well as a map for those on the journey to the writing life.

—Diana Norma Szokolyai
Cambridge, MA

MANIFESTOS

Plans

Richard Kenney

Weigh odds. Pray. Pay bills.
Tell truth. Love well. Serve real gods.
Meanwhile, daffodils.

Leaving My Former Life
Nell Irvin Painter

After my two toe-dipping Princeton painting classes, I took the summer drawing and painting marathon at the New York Studio School on 8th Street in Manhattan. The Studio School started at 9 a.m., ended at 6, with crits stretching past 9 p.m. For me that meant get up at 6 a.m., walk across the park, take Newark light rail to Newark Penn Station. New Jersey Transit to New York Penn Station, that hell of thank-you-for-your-patience dysfunction. The 2 or 3 subway downtown, get off at 4th Street, walk to 8th Street, and arrive before everyone else.

Then the pay-off. Stand up and draw and paint for eight hours. I loved it.

I L O V E D I T.

The paper, the charcoal, the canvas, the set-ups, the model, the space, the perspective, the shadows, the colors, the smell. Concentrating hard, I did it wrong, and I did it right. I painted a still life in red and blue that taught me that you can't mix cerulean blue from ultramarine and white oil paints as they come from a tube. A figure painting asked for warm but light browns for skin and an indefinite darker shade for light skin in shadow. This shade has no name, so you mix it out of the leavings on your palette.

Here's the best lesson of all from the Studio School marathon: Staple a 5' x 4' piece of tough watercolor paper to the wall; cover it with a charcoal drawing of the model in the set-up, the very best drawing you can make. Cover the entire paper. This takes hours standing up, drawing in the heat. Sweating. Now rub out your drawing with a chamois. Owwww!! All that work for nothing! Draw it again, only 10" to the right. Okay.

Concentrate. Draw. Sweat. Fill up the paper. Rub it out. Erase it again? Yes. Rub it out. Draw the model and set-up 1/3 smaller. Draw draw draw. Rub it out. Again.

Lesson learned? Essential lesson learned! You can erase what you draw, even what you've spent a long time drawing and sweating over. You can throw away what you paint and, as I learned to do later, cut it up and incorporate it into a new painting. A lesson to take straight to heart, and not only in art making.

I loved it. Even though I was the oldest by far, I stood up and painted right up until 6. Some of the kids came late, farted around, took two-hour lunch breaks, and left before dinner without washing their brushes. Crit came after dinner break. To accommodate Newark light rail's evening schedule, I would leave crit around 9 p.m. Start all over the next morning, five days a week. Okay, I could do it! Let's go!

You'll Never Be An Artist!

Nell Irvin Painter

You know, back in graduate school, I should have ignored my deficits. Even better, I should have flaunted them, making art according to my own bad-artist's hand, and lots of it, like a woman in the undergraduate painting class I had to take in the winter session of my first year. Sulking over my punishment, I envied her freedom over in the large corner she had commandeered and turned into her own personal studios.

Mary wasn't a regular RISD student. She was on the staff, taking a painting class just for the hell of it. No one was telling her to work on her skills. She fenced off her corner with piles of the work she made with a cadmium-red-hot-furious, total disregard. She made tons of work, most of it junk. But some of it grabbed you and would not let loose of your eyes. Some of it exploded with all energy she threw—and I do mean threw—into her paintings.

The rest of us in the class, mostly undergraduates, were dutifully painting studio set-ups with models and a collection of miscellaneous objects—tires, fishnet, pots, chairs, and fabrics—things famously hard to depict. I hated every last damned painting I made there, so stinking were they of art school set-ups. There I was, laboring like an undergraduate over verisimilitude, striving to capture the set-up, when I should have been, like Mary, painting what my hand was seeing. I was trying to paint as I thought I was supposed to in order to improve my skills. I hated hated hated every fucking moment in the studio in that class. Mary loved it with matching fervor.

Over in her corner, she painted, tore up her paintings, pasted them together in every which way, assignments be damned. To hell with the assignments! To hell with the blasted set-ups! Meanwhile, boring old me painted my stupid paintings by the rules. I'd never be an artist, never be An Artist. What would I be?

A TOTAL FAILURE

Hey! Not so fast. Not a total failure. One assignment, tapping into my old habit of painting myself, suited my eye and my hand. Sitting at the kitchen table in my apartment, I freely drew, painted, and collaged myself. We were to paint ten self-portraits 12 x 12". I made 25. I made them on paper and on board, as drawings, collages, and monoprints, in colors bright and subdued. They were all close-ups, but with varied backgrounds: landscapes, patterns, collage, and abstract. Okay. Twenty-five instead of ten of me me me. Best things ever at RISD. Who cares if I'm never An Artist artist.

I have never tried to make my self-portraits look like me, for issues of beauty and skin color and all the other judgment-laden markers of race and gender threaten to trip me up. I'm a nice-looking woman. What does it say if I paint myself as beautiful? My skin is dark. What if I made myself too dark or too light? What even counts as too dark or light?

Here lie snares for every black artist, for issues of skin color and nose shape and lip size and thickness and hair texture all carry positive and negative connotations in the aesthetics of race. They aren't just appearance, not just how things look. Every single line or volume carries social meaning. If I made my lips too thin or my color not dark enough, it could speak a lack of race pride. What about my hair? What a chore to try to depict it in its variegated nappiness, but how to capture it? Every single decision about self-representation could tip me into a racial morass.

My self-portraits wouldn't be just paintings of a particular individual rendered in a particular painting style. They entered a field of black-woman visual representation encompassing the beauty of Beyoncé and Michelle Obama, in which the light skin of the former fits easily into American tastes and the dark skin of the latter awakens new understandings while also attracting bigotry. "The black body" as mine field.

Black artists have myriad strategies for dealing with "the black body," for each individual black person's body, in this case, my own, exists within a visual field of pre-existing imagery, be it negative or positive. I had seen this first hand with my parents, who were seen differently with the passage of time. And I don't mean this in terms of age, but with regards to skin color and evolving beauty ideals.

My father had always been considered handsome—still was, deep into his 90s, his light skin according with American beauty standards, his good health and personal charm further heightening his attractiveness. My mother, a different story, and not only because for years she was so shy. Because of her dark skin, my mother never felt beautiful, even though she always was beautiful. Only in her maturity was she widely complimented, due not to a change in her appearance, but to a broadening of American beauty ideals. She was in her eighties when she quoted what people said to her as the title of her memoir: *I Hope I Look That Good When I'm That Old.* After black became beautiful in the 1960s, my mother's beauty became obvious. I watched that change, and it inspired my work on physical beauty, manifested in my Michael Jackson and Apollo Belvedere paintings. So, yes, when you see my paintings and my self-portraits, you're seeing reflections of my mother's emergence into beauty and my awareness of a nimbus of images and appearances around "the black body," mine as well as hers.

How to be a Writer
Elisabeth Sharp McKetta

Live a mother's life when with your daughter. Live a wife's life when with your husband. Live a monk's life every other minute of every day.

Eat vegetarian so that you can look all animals in the eye and feel empathy. Remember that empathy is a writer's greatest tool (second to it is self-trust, third the willingness to sit in the chair). Because empathy matters most, wake early to practice Tonglen Meditation.

Eat fat because it is good for the brain.

Simplify choices. You eat this way, you wear these colors. Frame your responsibilities. You see friends here, you write in the mornings, before exercise. Respect and repeat these frames. Observe them too, and every season or so, ask if they need change.

Recognize that you do not love mushrooms but your daughter and husband do. Give them your mushrooms.

Take retreats often. Every working morning is a retreat of sorts. Take longer ones too, every season or so. Leave town to go where the population is 63 and there is only one bakery. Write well and hard for six hours a day. Then relish coming home.

Finish projects when you say you will. This is part of self-trust. Finishing on time will also help you empathize with yourself and your writer's days. The bottom line to all of this is sitting in the chair.

Consider dedicating one work day every week to anything you wish to write. Have fun! Return the next day to the project you are going to finish.

Eat slowly, breathe deeply, read widely, love playfully, sleep long, and finish a new work every year. A big work. A work you want your people to read and read again.

Write credos when you must, but not too often. Best is to write them once a year, but if you cannot stand the wait, once a season or so.

Treat Your First Draft Like a One-Night Stand
Lillian Ann Slugocki

Treat your first draft like a one-night stand. Bring tequila, insanity, and animal instincts to the party—drape your panties on a bare light bulb, kick your shoes across the room, play loud music, dance naked. Drink too much, and throw up on the kitchen floor. Never, ever promise to return. And never say I love you. You won't be back, you're here for the thrill of it. And that is all.

You're not the voice of your generation, you're not writing the great American novel, you're not deconstructing *Ulysses*, or writing a memoir that finally and definitively encapsulates the 80's. You are not trying to define or expand upon your genre. You are just having fun. You are just fucking. Again, for the sheer thrill of it. You are writing because it fucking makes you feel alive.

Set the mood. Candles are excellent. French roast or cannabis? Vodka or madeleines? And please, consider your space. Fix it till it feels good. Ask your lover, *What kind of music do you like*, and then play what you like, even if it's the Sex Pistols, Madame Butterfly, Talking Heads, Donna Summer, Philip Glass, or Barry White because he says, "I don't want to feel no panties."

Do not worry about commitments. Set a deadline to finish, or don't. But whatever you do, don't obsess about structure, characters, mood, setting, voice, or tone—not to mention your social media platforms, your demographic, your key words, or your genre, in other words, a serious relationship. Because that is the very best way to ruin the fucking. Satisfaction not guaranteed. That will not be fun.

The first draft is a sloppy, sweating, sexy beast. Chaos abounds. So does bullshit. It should be a total disaster. Because the only thing that matters is finishing it—whatever it is; novel, novella, epic poem, collection, memoir, fable, fairy-tale, personal myth, and that's why you have to be stupid and careless. Wear cheap perfume, and ripped black underwear, scuffed boots and eye shadow. Don't bring your A-game, be like Kim Novak in *Picnic.* Fuck your reputation. Have fun.

Of course, you will be back. You will be back and you might even spend months, years, or decades with this lover. Mornings and evenings. Fall and winter. Deep in the hot heart of summer: Unwashed hair, nothing but peanut butter in the fridge, dirty dishes, dust, unopened mail, laundry spooling out from the closet, and it's 2:00 a.m., and you have to be up at 6:00 a.m. But you are back again, with this lover, who has long ceased to be a one-night stand.

On Memoir

Jade Sylvan

If you'd asked when I was twenty-five if I thought I'd ever write a memoir, I would have said "absolutely not." Memoir, as far as I saw it, was masturbation. Poetry and fiction held *real* truth. I didn't see any value at all in this type of navel-gazing. Who would want to read about *me*?

Besides, I was shy. Super shy. I'm a very queer, very kinky, very polyamorous genderqueer who grew up in a conservative Catholic family in a conservative Republican state. I was bullied a TON, and felt like I had to hide a lot of who I was from my community. I grew up with a lot of shame and learned how to disguise my inner world by turning it into safely disguised art. I used to write stories and poetry that were far, far away from me. It was much easier to write about the secrets in my heart in metaphors and allegories than concrete descriptions. A man who died after having sex with a horse was easier for me to write about than my own kinkiness. A pansexual vampire stripper was safer for me to imagine than to look honestly at my own pansexuality.

When I started to write more personally, I was terrified no one would be able to understand what I was saying. I was so used to feeling like a freak, a deviant, and an outcast. I was sure that writing autobiographically would lead to my being shunned. Surprisingly, the opposite happened. The more honestly and clearly I wrote about these intimate parts of myself, the more passionately people seemed to connect with my work. This reaction was beyond validating. Eventually, this honest, introspective roll led me to write a full-length memoir, *Kissing Oscar Wilde*, which was largely about my relationship to my sexuality.

Thing is, I wasn't wrong. Memoir *is* masturbation. When you write a memoir, you are stroking yourself, penetrating yourself, and exposing your innermost regions for your own perverse pain and pleasure. It is inherently self-absorbed and obsessed with private fetishes, desires, and embarrassments. Thing is, if you check out any internet porn site, you'll find that people love to watch other people masturbate.

When you publish a memoir, you enter into an exhibitionist/voyeur relationship with your readers. This is not for everyone, but some people truly do like to be watched. I found that the more I exposed the parts of myself that made me cringe, the happier I was. The more people loved and lauded me for these previously secret shames, the fuller I felt as a human being. Is this exhibitionistic? Sure it is. Is there anything wrong with that? Not at all.

A good memoir provides a private-yet-connected release to the writer and the reader. What makes a good memoir? Like porn, memoir works best when it's honest. Both the camgirl and the memoirist are most effective when they're having fun. So look deep inside, open up, and above all, don't fake it.

The Body of the Poem
Stephanie Burt

This essay first appeared in 2013. I stand by everything that it says about poems and poetry; as for the way in which I present myself, it's worth noting that I am simply Stephanie, and identify myself much more simply, as a transgender woman, now. I still, often, feel like more than one person—like many more than one person—inside, though, and I still think that feeling of multiplicity, as well as the feeling of mismatch between body and spirit or soul, is one of the feelings that poetry (even poetry by cisgender poets) exists to address.

Before we can think about transgender bodies, transgender writers, and our (perhaps) transgender poems, we will have to think about bodies and poems in general. I'll get back to trans people, and to our poems in particular, a few paragraphs down; if that's what you're seeking, stay with me.

By now it's a commonplace, though not a truth universally acknowledged, that a poem can stand in for, or create an alternative to, a human face and a human body: for the writer (after she writes it) and for the reader (while she is reading it). Jay Wright says that a poem creates a "body that stands apart from itself." Wallace Stevens, in "The Motive for Metaphor," suggests that literary figuration opens up, or imagines, a world "[o]f things that would never be quite expressed, / Where you yourself were never quite yourself / And did not want nor have to be."

And so unless the poem is a dramatic monologue—and maybe even when it is—the poet is both herself and not herself, or not quite herself; the poem augments her face, or substitutes for it. Think of Emily Dickinson's poem, so often taught to children, that begins "I'm Nobody—who are you?" Think of the people in Randall Jarrell's late poems, often middle-aged women, who want nothing so much as to be noticed, to be seen: "The world goes by my cage and never sees me," says one. Think of Rainer Maria Rilke's "Archaic Torso of Apollo," whose sacred headless sculpture (a figure for poetry) seems to meet our gaze, to speak to us, even though we can never see its face. Or think of Shakespeare's sonnet 83: "I never saw that you did painting need / And therefore to your fair no painting set," where "painting" means word-painting (flattering poetic description), portrait painting (preserving a face through art) and the morally suspect artfulness of cosmetics (improving the face you have by applying makeup). The poet would have made a better face, a more durable face, for the beloved, but felt he could not, because the beloved's real face is as good as it gets.

We need poetry when literal faces and bodies and circumstances are *not* as good as it gets: we might enjoy reading and writing poetry for many reasons, but we *need* it when we feel that we need figuration, need something unavailable in the literal world. That "something" might be a theodicy, a way "to justify the ways of God to man," it might be an expression of grief, or devotion, or confusion, or frustration. But it might also be a new face, a new body; it might be a way to make the inward person audible (if not visible) to other people, if the outward person cannot match what's inside.

And it never wholly does. All of us are, like *Doctor Who*'s TARDIS, bigger on the inside than on the outside. Few of us are finished, none of us ever find moments when we have at last enunciated the single, true, real, authentic, satisfactory self: instead, we can work to articulate that self as it changes and multiplies and evades us, whether or not we do so with our changing bodies' physical appearance, whether or not we do it in poems. "Who doesn't want / to be called something / other than the name we're given?" writes the contemporary poet Angie Estes. Nobody ever feels that even her closest friends know all of her, all the time, at any one time, and it only gets worse (we get more opaque) if we consider ourselves *in* time, since who I am now can obscure whatever I have been. Another contemporary poet, Laura Kasischke, writes that "growing older" is like being "blindfolded, walking // straight through one / immaterial mirror / and into another. / But it's never enough." You never see, you can never get other people to see, or hear, all of yourself: no one face, no one text, can suffice, no matter who you think you are.

These questions—of poetry and voice, of visibility and self-consciousness, of textual faces and textual substitute bodies—apply to all poems, but they have special salience when the bodies and the poet in question are trans or genderqueer. Definitions may be in order here. Trans people are people whose inner sense of gender—of whether and when we are men, women, boys or girls—does not match either our anatomical sex, or our former anatomical sex, or the way in which other people have seen us. The category includes sometime cross-dressers, performing drag kings and drag queens, people who change their everyday full-time gender—before, during, after, or without surgeries— and some people who are biologically intersex (other intersex people reject the term). "Cisgender"—a back-formation, like "acoustic guitar"—refers to people who are not trans: whose sense of their own gender matches their social role and biological sex. People who label themselves as genderqueer are trying to queer (or "trouble," or bend, or break) the binary of gender, to live as both/and or as neither/nor.

I, for example, love to be called Stephanie, though I first asked somebody to call me by that name less than two years ago. I wish I were a woman—or a girl—often, and I might be Stephanie all the time if it were easier. I'm happy enough as Stephen, most of the time, and I'm lucky to find social acceptance when I dress as a woman just now and then, and to play with the signifiers of gender, around their margins, in the rest of my life. The terms "trans" and "transgender" thus include me, while "transsexual" does not, nor does "drag queen" (which implies a stage act); "transvestite" sounds dated (it also sounds like a rare mineral), and "cross-dresser," while accurate, has the unfortunate implication that I'm interested mostly (or fetishistically) in clothes.

Don't get me wrong: I *am* interested in clothes. With the right women's clothes, I can feel that I am more myself, even that I am better than myself, a Stephanie who is prettier and more confident than the Stephen I have historically been. I like learning about women's clothes, and about makeup too, and I wish I had learned a lot more a lot sooner. I know it's not worth it to me—it would be too disruptive, both practically and emotionally, to me and to people around me—for me to live as Stephanie full time, but I also know that I would like to be able to use women's clothes more often, more fully, more deftly, as a means of self-expression: as a way to feel pretty, to be both the person I am and the people whom I would like to be.

"People," not "person." I would, in fact, like to be several mutually incompatible women and girls: a techie tomboy; a confident professional woman whose palette is grey, gold and black; a girl who in several senses has not quite developed, who still puts hearts on her "i's"; a reviver of colorblock tops, bringing back the New Wave. I would like to resemble the British pop star Clare Grogan, and the cute starship mechanic from the TV show *Firefly*, and Katherine Hepburn, none of whom resemble each other, and Kitty Pryde from *X-Men*, who doesn't exist. I would also, at times, like to be, and I can see myself vividly as if I were, a point guard, and a ferret, and (like Shelley and Mayakovsky before me) a cloud. Sometimes I feel that I might as well be seventy-five years old; sometimes I feel that I'm "really" twelve.

Some of those identities can be approximated, approached, even if clumsily, with makeup and wardrobe; some of them can't, or not for me. But all of them could be, and some of them have been, explored in my own poems. I think (I have no way of knowing) that if I had been born a girl and had grown up a woman I would still have a profession in one of the arts that use words; I might even be a professor and a literary scholar and a cultural critic, doing much of what I do now. But I am not sure that I would have become a poet, not sure that I would have had the same motivation to make these odd, embarrassing, risky, intuitive, apparently useless art forms that can stand in for the bodies and faces we have, to eclipse or disguise the literal with *figura*, with artifice made up of language alone.

My goals as a poet overlap with the goals of the 54 other poets included along with me in *Troubling the Line: Trans and Genderqueer Poetry and Poetics*, a recent anthology edited by TC Tolbert and Tim Trace Peterson. A prose statement by one contributor, Jen (Jay) Besemer (the parentheses in the name are Besemer's own), speaks, perhaps inadvertently, to the head-turning range of the anthology as a whole:

Some poems look like informational captions for photos taken by stone-age cameras. Some poems take the form of bibliographic citations. Some wear the clothes of word problems on standardized tests. Are you a man or a woman? Are you a door or a window?...Sometimes I appear evasive or contrary so as to avoid miscategorizing myself… What I am is how I work and what I make.

Besemer's statement also has the virtue of humor: "I was female when I was born. Later additional information became available."

This big book includes cross-dressers, like me, and others who live in two genders but won't transition; people, such as the Michigan poet J. Rice, who are writing during transition; transmen and transwomen who have transitioned, such as Joy Ladin and Samuel Ace; and people for whom it's more complicated. It has writers already eminent, either nationally (Eileen Myles) or within a queer avant-garde (the late kari edwards), and writers for whom it's their first appearance in print. It's also got people working in and through and against several other identity categories—among them heritage language, race, disability, fat pride, Deaf culture, and early abuse—and people whose poems draw on poetic lineages, on styles and goals, that are far from my own.

In particular—that is, particularly far from what I think I do—are people who seem to be writing for performance, in front of an audience, in their own body, in real time, however gendered or attired. That's an art form that comes close to the one that I practice, but it's also disturbing and alien to me, because it seems to insert back into "poetry" the very things—the physical body of just one person at a particular moment in space and in time—that "poetry," for me, attempts to escape. I am happy to read my poems in public: overjoyed (if also nervous) to read them as Stephanie, delighted to read them as Stephen in a T-shirt and jeans, and willing to put on a tie if the venue demands. What's alien to me is the idea that my poems somehow *require* my bodily presence, in real time (as if a musical composition were pointless unless you had seen it performed live).

But maybe, for these performance poets, the integration of person and poem, of writer, reciter and text, is part of the point. A performance poet who makes queer identity his or her or hir or their subject is integrating the personae that come from the poetry into the living body attached to the poet's name: and that sort of integration is what, to me, seems impossible or undesirable, either because it's impossible in general (each of us "hath that within which passeth show") or because it's impossible for me.

Troubling the Line required author photos from all contributors: they take up a third of a page, with each author's first poem. Usually I dislike author photos, since they encourage us to judge by appearances. Here, however, the author photos are great, because they remind us that the poems are part of a project by which trans people try to make space in the world where we can show more, feel free to be more, of ourselves. "There is something important," writes Peterson, "about the relation-ship between how trans poets look and how they *look* (at the world, at language), between how they read and how they want to be read (or to be unreadable)." "Read" here has an additional special meaning, since to be "read" is to be identified, especially by a stranger, as trans. (If you are not "read," you can "pass": be seen as a cisgender woman or man.) To be out as a trans poet is to be visible: it is, in this sense, to want to, to try to, be read.

In addition to the photographs, Peterson and Tolbert also required each contributor (other than the two now deceased) to provide an origi-nal statement of "poetics," in prose. Some of the poets who don't quite move me with their own poems make me sit up and take note with their statements. My own poetics statement, written two years ago, now seems defensive, over-cautious, afraid to be taken the wrong way: I didn't want people to think I was "going full-time" (living as a woman from day to day), much less to think I was leaving my wife and children, and I didn't understand (yet) how to write with any confidence about being both-and, neither-nor, Stephen-and-Stephanie, except in disguise and in poems. I think I'm slightly better at it now. As I read through the other poets' prose statements, I find myself asking, not just how well I think each poet handles the language, but whether the life that the poets claim to represent, to re-embody, to voice, is or is not anything like mine.

My answers make me feel very white; they also make me realize that I feel much closer to the writers who identify as butch or as female-to-male (FTM)—who want to be manly, or to be men, even more than I want to be a woman or a girl—than I feel to the writers who want to destroy gender entirely. As with the rest of our social and political and verbal life, so with gender in language: I don't think that we can just smash everything and start over, but rather that we need to use all the tools we can find in order to open up and repair and improve what we have.

I feel closest, of course, to the writers who want to be feminine, or female, or women, or girls. To J. Rice, whose wife has been watching her transition:

> This morning before
> the mirror I said *These*
> *are my breasts* and you
> looked away in disgust
> and silence. All winter
> you insist I've been two
>
> people.

If I have read the poem rightly, Rice herself sees her transition, instead, as a process by which she turns from two people into one. "For the first 30 years of my life," Rice writes in her prose statement, "I escaped my body most through writing, which became the most recognizable and liveable space I knew." (As it did for Stevens; as it can for me.) Rice now writes instead from within a positive feedback loop: "If I admit who I am, who will I become?" It's a fear that I've had during what I am now willing to call the coming-out process, too.

Despite the usual problems with such events (too many writers, not much time for each), the marathon reading for *Troubling the Line* during the AWP conference in Boston in March 2013 was the first marathon reading that I've ever enjoyed, because it was a chance to claim an identity. Whether I liked individual poems, or individual performances, wasn't nearly as important as the fact that we could share—that I, as Stephanie, could share—that space. It's not a feeling I need every day, but it is one I want very much from time to time. Right now, at least, Stephen needs Stephanie, because I am her, and Stephanie needs the solidarity with other trans and genderqueer artists that an anthology like *Troubling the Line* turns out to provide.

I had an almost comically hard time physically reaching that Boston reading, walking to its site: one of my heels almost broke, I kept stepping in puddles, I got the address badly wrong, and I felt as if something or someone did not want me to get my body to this assembly of people whose bodies informed our work. Once I got there I knew I was (a) a bit late and (b) welcome. The room ended up being almost full—there were perhaps a hundred people: I saw at least as many transmen and butch people and genderqueer young people with short asymmetrical hair as I did people who looked feminine, or who were trying to look feminine, like me; the range of readers matched the range of the book.

I had complicated reactions to the Boston reading; it wasn't all joy and communion. It saddened me when I saw a few transwomen, or cross-dressers, who could not keep up a femme look, or did not know how to try: it's possible that people think of me that way, when I'm *en femme*. I was bored, occasionally, by all too straightforward verse about identities lost and found, verse I would have ignored were its subject almost anything else. But the reading also let me delight in seeing at least one femme author I'd never encountered before, both because she looked great, and because *Troubling the Line* turns out to be her first national appearance in print. That author is Lilith Latini, of Asheville, North Carolina, a ravishing, raven-haired studio-era femme fatale. (This is the first time I have ever written a sentence for publication about how a poet looked when she read her poems.) Those poems, raw as they could be, spoke to my twinned and antithetical desire for glamor and for solidarity, my wish to stand with others and my wish to stand out. It's not a wish unique to LGBT people, but it sounds great when Latini finds it in the thoughts of Stonewall queens: "Don't send me / out of the closet and into the streets alone. / Someone has to help me out of my strappy shoes before I run."

What is a "trans poem?" It might be any poem by a trans poet (the way "Irish poetry," for example, refers to poetry by Irish poets); it might, instead, be any poem that gives an account of life or thought or voice or language in more than one gender (in two, in three, in one-half). (What about poems whose speakers are women, but whose authors are non-trans-identified men—like

Jarrell, or Alexander Pope, or Ovid—or, vice versa, women who write for the voices of men? To include them all would be ahistorical; to exclude them all might leave out something valuable for transgender writing today.)

What if trans poems have to be self-consciously trans: to reflect awareness of the label on the part of an implied author? To reflect not only a voice or a persona that crosses or confuses gender, but an implied author who set out to do so, in dialogue with a modern, named identity? That's the definition of trans poetry that emerges from *Troubling the Line*, and it serves the book well. The anthology works not only as a set of explorations for what trans poetics might mean, but also as a coming-out party for an identity category, a set of people (myself among them) who are exploring an identity that a person (not only a poem) can have.

In theory, we could sort out three kinds of trans poetry: one kind would describe life in more than one gender at once, or life in a range of gendered personae, whether or not that life had a narrative arc; another kind would imply a narrative of departure, passage, and arrival, from one gender to another (especially apt for transsexual people); a third kind— analogous to third-gender or genderqueer lives—would attempt to destroy the binaries of gender entirely, to fashion a voice and a style outside or beyond them.

In practice, as I read through *Troubling the Line*, that three-part distinction turns out to be hard to maintain; nor do familiar distinctions among kinds of trans people (transsexuals, butches, third-gender people, etc.) map very well onto forms and styles for trans poems. Some of the poets in *Troubling the Line* are obviously MTF, some clearly third-gender, some obviously FTM, but part of the fun—and part of the cumulative effect of its contributors' diverse, often disorienting techniques—is that sometimes, from the poems, you can't quite tell. Aimee Herman's prose poem asks about itself, or about Herman's self, what we might ask about the whole collection: "How to define the need to not be defined." Herman continues:

> On Monday see Poet in tie and vest. On Tuesday, feast eyes upon cleavage and whale fat lipstick. On Wednesday Poet is packing, Poet is binding, Poet is gender concealed… I know I have long hair but sometimes I am boy. When I talk about my

dick I need you to believe that I have one [sometimes].

Herman would like to be both-and: to be one thing on one day, one thing on another, either for reasons of social mobility, awkwardness and convenience (it would be too hard for Herman to present as male all the time), or because that's simply how Herman feels. Ari Banias, on the other hand, would apparently like to be neither/nor. Banias's poem "Here's the Story on Being" reminds me of Jarrell's unhappy women, trapped in their overlooked bodies:

> and then a person addresses themselves to you—
> well, to your clothes,
> but I only borrowed these, you want to say, they aren't
> me, or you'd like to explain yours were broken or wet or
> you didn't have a skin—but it wouldn't make sense.

Most of the poets in *Troubling the Line* appear to agree (with me and with one another) that a poem and its form have something to do with the poet's body, and also that poetry can provide imagined alternatives to that literal body. "Consider the poem itself as a body, an extension of the writer," Ely Shipley suggests. "Every time I write a poem I make a little body," writes Oliver Bendorf, citing D.A. Powell. "Then I name it … and then maybe other people read it … My poem-bodies are inexact. They are sometimes uncertain of their hips on the page. Sometimes their voices crack." "The voice wants to turn itself into a body," Peterson writes:

> It can't, though it tries hard—
> it brings you flowers, to engender a meaningful
> relationship. It makes you coffee in the morning. Here, have a cup.

My voice wants to be a body, to be bodies, too, but it also wants to be … not the body I have. By writing poetry, by working in disembodied language, I can get out of the physical body I happen to have, can depict and counter the insufficiencies of the merely physical world; I can create other bodies for myself in words, some called Stephanie (or Kitty Pryde, or Kermit the Frog, or a lightbulb, or a hermit crab), some just called "I." But I have to stay within, have to acknowledge the limits, of a real world from which words and sentences come, and to which—however fictionalized, however figural—they refer.

Not everyone does. *Troubling the Line* has a high proportion of poems that use the unstable language of contemporary "experiment." They try to get away from the specific boxes and types and assumptions that come with *male, female, man, woman, boy, girl* by getting away from boxes and types and assumptions in general. "Clear the fascism of anxiety that begets identity begets narrative begets a story," urges Samuel Ace. Such writing does not want to cross a line, but to crumple it up, or erase it.

When I read the weaker "experimental" poems in this inspiring anthology, I feel lost; I do not know where I am. But that sense of lostness, or of sudden freedom, might be the point. Patriarchal and heteronormative and cisgender-normative assumptions underpin so many of our habits, in our language, in our economy, in our visual culture, in so much of our life, that a feminist queer genderqueer or trans-activist poet might well declare war against habits as such; might want to build up a new system, as if from scratch. I do not think that project, in its purest forms, can succeed; but I take pleasure in seeing and hearing other poets try.

For my part, I think that we take what we have and build on it, even if we flee from it as well. Whether or not its author is transgender, a poem is always an alternate self, an imaginary body, a form of transport: we make it from what we are and from what we know, from our immediate lived experience, from the examples we find in others, from what the culture and its words can give.

In this sense, *Troubling the Line* shows not just what all its trans writers share with one another, but how trans writing can illuminate one purpose of imaginative writing in general. Czeslaw Milosz wrote that "in the very essence of poetry there is something indecent, / a thing is brought forth that we didn't know we had in us." I agree. The same poem by Milosz announces that "the purpose of poetry is to remind us/ how difficult it is to remain just one person." There I think he was half-right: it seems to me that another purpose of poetry—especially, but not only, trans poetry—is to show us that we don't have to be.

Concerning Your Intentions as a Poet
Sam Cha

Dear Lloyd:

I once heard Robert Pinsky say, in a workshop, that he doesn't like to repeat himself, that he wants to do things he hasn't done before, and I suppose I'm in line with that. If there's been a constant for me as far as writing goes, I think it's to be found in my attempts to find new ways to write: shorter lines, longer lines, lines broken, lines staggered. Coherent viewpoint, fractured viewpoint. First person singular, first person plural. Five-year-old voice, thirty-two-year-old voice. Old forms, invented forms, non-forms. Maybe this is because I'm always afraid that I'm not going to be able to write anything that's any good or true or new. Maybe it's because, for me, poetry is about trying to invent a way to talk about what can't be talked about. "Whereof we cannot speak, thereof we must remain silent," says Wittgenstein. Von Hofmannstahl's Lord Chandos loses all confidence in language. Everyday objects glow with meaning, flash some kind of glory (unutterable, literally), but he can't make any of it stay. Language leaks. Kleist reads Kant, despairs of ever reaching capital-tee-Truth, caps himself. The "celestial light," "the glory and the freshness" always escapes Wordsworth. (Roadrunner, Coyote) "Every day is like Sunday," says Morrissey, "every day is silent and gray." "And no birds sing," Keats might say, or Spicer. Nevertheless they all kept speaking for a while, every man Jack and Stephen and William and Heinrich and Hugo and Ludwig. Why? "I can't go on, I'll go on," says Beckett.

So they keep soldiering on, stop and go, stop, and go, stop, and, go. "Often my language is nothing but stuttering," says Wittgenstein. Begin, end, begin. "Beginning again and again is a natural thing even when there is a series," says Stein. "Yawp," says Whitman. "MOVE, INSTANTER," says Olson. "I HATE SPEECH," says Grenier, but I think he's lying. Speech is broken (maybe), but it's all we've got, and it's the broken-ness of language that makes it fun, after all, the way rules apply here but not there, the way in logic if A != B they're never identical, but in metaphor

A can be B even when it's not; because it's not. (It is fun because we are in love with it. We are in love with it because it is broken.) It's the stuttering, the repetition of sound, the swerve of the sounds, all the phonemes falling straight down but then some of them ever so slightly moving slant ("Tell all the truth, but tell it slant," says Dickinson), and colliding and bouncing and cohering and breaking, until from that suddenly there's order, there's voice, there's rhythm, there's story, even (all this from Lucretius and his mildly obscene-sounding clinamen)—the cussed exuberance of it, coming from silence ("The foul rag and bone shop of the heart," says Yeats): I think that's the best thing I know. Which is why I try. On, off, begin, end, off, on, go on, go.

Hope that made sense?

Sam

The First Four Steps

Caitlin Johnson

One: You Must Read

It isn't enough to want to tell stories. Every writer is, above all, a reader. If you ever hear someone swear he doesn't read, be suspicious of anything he writes.

Ray Bradbury's philosophy was that you should fill yourself up with as much as possible, because the more words you consume, the more likely you are to know what works, what doesn't; what's been done, what hasn't; what kind of writer you want to be, what kind you don't. And never underestimate the effect someone else's words might have on you. They may spur you to greatness. But you won't know if you don't read their work.

For this reason, I tend to seek out a wide variety of titles, from celebrity memoirs to classic young adult works, contemporary poetry to historical biographies, and anything else that catches my eye. Even when a book isn't doing it for me, I try not to give up on it, because finishing it helps me better understand what I dislike about the work, and also helps encourage me to power through my own drafts when I feel I'm on the wrong track. To put it another way, we must practice a sort of fortitude that we may not apply in other areas of our lives in order to learn something about our writing.

Two: You Must Write

There are writers who say it is necessary to write every day for X number of hours (one, five, ten, etc.). I'm not the kind of person who prescribes a definite time span for writing, but I am also not the kind of person who believes in waiting for inspiration to strike.

Sure, jot some notes when a line of dialogue occurs to you. But make sure that you also sit yourself down to produce actual paragraphs. Or—if you're lucky—whole pages. If nothing is coming to you, edit. If you have nothing to edit (and let's face it—you do have things to edit), send your work out to journals and magazines. Writing is about more than the physical act; it's also necessary to advance your work, and I count that as writing time.

When it seems the muse (or whatever) has abandoned you, have a list of ideas handy to jump-start the process. My version of this is a note on my phone where I collect words I'd like to use in poems, opening sentences for short stories, and topics for blog posts. As a result, I am able to put myself in the zone, as it were, at any moment.

Three: You Must Sleep

Sleep is essential to our physical, mental, and emotional health. I believe it is also a necessary task in the writer's life.

All sorts of weird stuff goes down in your brain while you slumber. Dreams sometimes turn into fantastic stories, because they can show you things you wouldn't conjure up during waking hours. Landscapes, characters, and situations arise in dreams that may help you take your novel or poem to a higher level of awesome. But the best part about sleep is undoubtedly the fact that you can rest up and brace yourself to face another day, another story, another deadline.

Since I was an adolescent, I've had a recurring dream about my grandmother's house—or, at least, what my brain tells me is my grandmother's house, which barely resembles the actual thing but embodies the spirit of the place. I hope to examine in an essay how this dream has evolved over the years as family members have come and gone and our lives have changed. Other dreams might provide the start of other pieces, as well.

Four: You Must Fall in Love

This is the most important step.

"What I love," Sylvia Plath wrote in *Years*, "is / The piston in motion— / My soul dies before it." What I love is the feeling I get when someone reads my words and connects with them. This is the thing that sustains me through the writing of the next poem or story: the validation that comes along with putting my own soul into my work and touching someone else's life as a result.

To be a writer, you have to love words. You have to love the world. You have to love the possibility of the blank page and the audience. Without that passion and adoration, you won't get far in your writing.

Poet, Try:
Some Notes on Writing and Teaching

Christine Johnson-Duell

I. Eye, Ear, Word

Once, I was part of a teaching team that led an intro to poetry class for undergraduates. We draped the structure of the class over Pound's *phanopoeia*, *melopoeia*, and *logopoeia*: eye, ear, word. Or, eye/ear/word. Or, "eyeearword."

For me, these three are the fundamental pieces of a poem. A poem needs all of them, working together. They are my guides when I write poems and the poems I love always have these three elements. Together, they comprise my three-legged stool of poetry. A piece of writing that calls itself a poem and yet lacks one of these elements is probably going to be a little wobbly.

Poems certainly have other elements in them but I believe they spring from the interplay between and coalescence of eye, ear, and word.

II. Rules

Form—the shape in which a poet builds her poem—holds together eye, ear, and word.

In high school, when I learned that Frost characterized free verse as akin to "playing tennis without a net," I thought, "Great! No rules! That's for me!"

Not quite. Even without a net, we're still playing tennis, so we need some rules. Sometimes, if he or she is playing tennis without a net, a poet has to invent rules, so the poem has a shape.

When I teach poetry to young children, rules are the second thing we discuss.

The kids and I mark the beat in Frost's *Stopping by Woods*...or Yeats's *Song of the Wandering Aengus*. We don't mark willy-nilly. We make agreements. Will we stomp? Snap our fingers? Clap our hands? Will we make this racket inside or outside? Walking in a circle? Sitting in a circle? Marching in a line? On our own or together?

We define and agree on the boundaries—the rules, if you will—we're going to observe because that's what poets do. Poets follow the rules. Poetry wants rules. Kids and poets understand rules: why we have them, and how it feels to break them.

In the undergraduate "Beginning Verse Writing" class, in which I was a TA, I gave a lecture about form. I began with the example of 1-4-5 blues, a restrictive musical form. Its restriction sets up an expectation—a form—that blues musicians follow, but the hallmark of blues is improvisation. The best blues players and singers riff on the rules.

Skilled poets, like skilled musicians, know the rules so well they know where and how to break them. And, breaking the rules can be very interesting.

III. Mystery

Contrary to what Auden said, poetry makes something happen. Poems elicit emotion. (They don't usually describe it.)

The etymology of the word "poem" is "to make, to create." Poetry makes something new out of its recognizable parts (its parts being the words we already know, rhythms that are in our bodies).

The first thing I do when I teach poetry to young children is this:

I write "POETRY" on the board.

I ask: "What's the word in a word here? What word is hiding inside 'poetry'?" And the kids love to find the word POET. Or, TRY.

It's best to let them find the words themselves. Telling them won't do, because the finding, the "Aha!" moment of making a connection, of making something out of nothing—out of what existed, until recently, outside your experience—is, possibly, the best and most compelling answer to the question, "why poetry?" Why read it? Why write it? Well, the kids might say "Poet, just try."

Manifesto: Aphorisms on Poetry
Thade Correa

The world is a continually-unfolding dream made of desire, never complete, never to be completed. Endless voyage. The world is poetry.

*

We are worlds, are worlds-within-worlds made of dream, made of desire. Endless voyagers. We are poetry.

*

Art is born of a place beyond signification, beyond words, and communicates to a place beyond words. Poetry is the struggle to say the unsayable, the use of words to reach beyond words, into the heart of an experience, into the heart of being. Poetry is the primordial song—or cry, or shout—of the human soul. Or, to put it as Yves Bonnefoy does, "Poetry is that which tries to make music of what occurs in life."

*

Before everything: silence. Then the ache of being, the cry of being. And then the singing.

*

I have always felt keenly aware of the limitations of language. The composer Claude Debussy wrote, "Music is the silence between the notes." Likewise, poetry is the space between the words. Just as a piece of music is not reducible to the notes that compose it, a poem is not reducible to the words on the page. Poetry comes from the void and reaches into the void, the Openness that is overflowing with infinite possibility, infinite meaning, and infinite life—and with numinous, ineffable experience.

*

Art is of the Moment, not of time.

*

Poetry is when thought becomes action, word becomes existence, image becomes experience, silence becomes song.

*

To do now, rather than wait. Only poetry can save at all times. But we must believe in it.

*

To give life to stones. Whether stones are inherently alive or we ascribe life to them does not matter. Our power to create gives life to stones. Stones also give life to us.

*

Living, in all its brokenness, incomprehensibility, meaninglessness, and chaos, is the greatest gift and sacrament. In its difficulty lies its wonder, and in its chaos and resistance to meaning lies its potential to encompass every meaning. Poetry is meaningless, as life is meaningless. Poetry calls upon the universe itself to create its meaning according to the Moment and weather.

*

The meaningfulness of all things—that they may be filtered through myself, and become my meaning.

*

Art's emptiness: in its uselessness is its highest use.

*

To think with materials, to let the universe be without ideas. To allow form to happen. To make magic with the things of the earth. The poet as shaman, the poem as experience itself, not a presentation of it. Art not as mimicry but as Newness itself: what was once an uncreated nothingness suddenly becomes incarnate, embodied. Poetry as existence made manifest in words.

*

The poem as sky, not mirror.

*

Poetry, the sacred wilderness, the always-present Eleusis, the void out of which tumbles the world.

*

Poetry, the Openness in which swim the minds of the gods.

*

Poetry, whose remembrance frees the body, whose forgetting chains the mind.

*

Poetry, vestigial human wings, forgotten.

*

The act of creation in not always simply positive. To learn the patience to let the voice lie silent until its time—for in silence the soul lies in the stillness and tumult of death, that is, the death that is really life illumined. To learn that to be silent is to create silence. It is better to speak one word that is right and then wait for that word to die in the air, that it may be changed into the sky and infinity, than to speak a thousand words without awareness.

*

Bathed in darkness, we can continue on in the light.

*

Artaud proclaimed: "The body has invented the soul." We must work to create a life in which it is possible to believe in what we desire to believe in. The physical nature of faith—the birth of god through the body. We must labor to bear the dream incarnate. This is the Work.

*

The possibility that a life may be lived that has never been lived before, that a world may be created that has never existed—this is our gift, every day.

*

Nothing has been completely revealed.

*

A prison only reveals the truest freedom—it does not bind, it releases.

*

The universe broken is still the universe; the empty sky contained in an open window is still empty forever.

*

To be blessed by being shattered.

*

At the end of all work, all striving, we must know that nothing is greater than to exist, to be in the living air a meaning, a deep sky, a season of the cosmos, a world within the World. To say, with Ezra Pound:

"Do not move
   let the wind speak
      that is paradise." (Canto CXX)

*

Poetry, the impossible eternity of momentary and disappearing gestures.

*

The Moment, healer of time.

The Gloaming

Molly Sutton Kiefer

Six months ago...

It's night. I haven't written in months, nothing that zings out of me anyway. My fingers itch—it feels as if there are fireflies residing in my joints. They are the light from which I write; they are the glow. It's strange to feel myself on pause like this. I am still breathing, I know— but where has the rest of it gone?

*

When I'm on, I write from every moment. The most prominent are those ones when pen-and-paper are unrealistic. The shower: I've learned to hum the lines, cycle and cycle as I build the routine of hair washing and body scrubbing. Driving: my husband gave me a handheld tape recorder to keep me from veering off the road. Once, I spoke a few lines about deer and their pink roadkill X's. I lost the recorder and the poem. Falling asleep: isn't this the most delicious time? I love falling asleep. I love closing the door on a good day, a day I've *done something*. The laundry might even be put away. I've taken to leaving print-outs of discarded manuscripts by the side of the bed, writing by the light of my cell phone. These are the drafts that make it to a second draft the most often. Sometimes, I swear I'll remember it in the morning. I never do.

*

An exercise: steal a line. Steal a first line, a last line. Steal a title. Write.

*

When my poet-friends fall silent, I tell them: *Trust your process. Trust the journey.* Easy for me to say; I don't mind carrying my writing notebook with me wherever I go. It will earn its place in my satchel; I will write something at some point in the day.

*

One of my closest friends went to Oregon for a spring while her husband worked a guest spot at a tattoo shop. She'd write to me of going for long walks outside; I'd imagine her as the landscape changed, high-stepping over dried out grasses, her dog galumphing beside her. She said she was "filling her well," a phrase we toted from Julia Cameron.

Her night: outside, it rained. Inside, she built fires. She waited.

*

Letting the well fill implies a kind of patience I'm not sure I have. *Go forth, fill your well!* I could say to a friend while cursing my own for not filling instantly. Hyperbolic hypocrite. We are in an instant-culture, and I am the best of the impulse buyers. Set those tables up with tchotchkes, and I will fill my pockets.

*

Three years ago…

It's night. I have to finish my thesis manuscript. I had a baby a few months ago—a 42-hours-of-labor/C-section-in-the-end baby. I had a baby who came out of a gaping wound in my belly and she nurses long and well. I wake at all hours to fill her sweet baby belly, and I've taken to puttering downstairs after, taking a shower, writing a new poem. In this way, I finish my thesis, one milk-wet poem at a time.

*

An exercise:

Take a poem you love—yours, or by someone else—and try to write an exact opposite poem. Write it with the same bones—situation, narrative—but give it a different form with a different attitude. This poem is calm? Write a hyped up poem. Write an *angry poem!* See how form informs the changed attitude.

*

In April and into May of 2013, I had a strange convergence of creative energy: I participated in Tupelo Press's 30/30 Project, which meant writing a poem-a-day in a fundraising marathon; I finished my time with the Loft Literary Center's Mentorship Program; and I wrote a book. An entire book in the briefest of surges, a startling and ambitious period of time.

And when it was done, I promptly fell silent.

*

See how words can transform themselves, become others: *fill -> fell -> well.*

*

I did not write from June of 2013 until January of 2014. In this time, my father-in-law passed away, my son learned to walk. We had Christmas. I sewed seventeen memorial bears out of old T-shirts. I knit. I bought a quilting machine.

I put away drafts of poems.

*

An exercise: write a poem in the form of a recipe.

*

I accept the statement: *I don't believe in writer's block.* If writer's block means not knowing what to write about, yes, I agree. Our lives are filled with material.

What I find most difficult is getting into a writerly mode.

*

As I write this, my son is inserting goldfish crackers into the gaps between his toes at my feet. I'm pretty sure that earthy smell coming from the kitchen means our clung leftovers in the sink are composting.

So how to get out of the starting block? I'm here. I showed up, at this page.

*

Poet Oliver de la Paz described his routine to the Loft mentees: often he'll give himself twenty minutes or so to revise old poems. The door is shut, no goldfish puppet show for him. The time with previous drafts gives him that much-needed transition from The World Out There to The World in Here.

*

I bought myself a spiral bound set of index cards. Each time I come up with an idea (*write a persona poem from the perspective of Jocasta; write a poem that uses architecture as its modeling structure/form*), I jot it. When I find a stolen moment, I can flip through—Rolex-flip it—write. Poetic recipe cards.

*

An exercise:

Begin collecting all of your favorite words. Put them on little slips of paper. Collect and collect, bird-making-a-nest. Spread them out on your table and write—try to add as few words as possible, but adjust—make nouns into verbs, shush them into place. Let your eyes do the directing, create pretty little poem nuggets.

*

It is night. I am too tired to write. I've had it somewhere, in the pit of me, all day, but still—the children sleeping, their little toes twitching in happy puppy-dreams—it's all I can do to keep myself from burying my face in the covers. Peel open a book instead. It's night and I need to rest.

*

My best way of transitioning into poetry-mode is to *read poetry*. There are some poets who can do it for me all the time. I will read some of their poems, and I will immediately need to write my own take. They will mention a train and suddenly I am writing about the year we lived a lot away from the tracks. There will be an oversized puddle and I am writing about collecting tadpoles in the culvert by our house. I see it as pinging of light, as if there is a single act of pinball—that *ting!* And I am off, elsewhere, writing.

*

An exercise:

Go for a walk. Fill your pockets with things you find. Write a natural narrative.

*

My friend, who was back into The Quiet, as I've often called it (though it's never felt still to me), asked me how I got out this time. I know she wanted me to tell her something magical, but I couldn't.

On a listserv, one mother mentioned her son's taking a semester off school, creating a reading list and discussing Joyce at the dinner table. I remembered myself as a high-schooler, ambitious, wanting to write books. It surged awake in me.

I don't understand triggers. I don't know that I need to.

I just need to know how to ride them.

*

Another poet-friend of mine sends a letter, telling me about her brother who is dying. I tell her: *write through it*. It needn't be carefully sculpted poems.

Just write, keep the pen moving.

When my father-in-law was in hospice, I wrote one poem.

When my grandfather was dying of Alzheimer's, I wrote a new poem every day.

I do not understand why the two are different. Do I need to?

*

An exercise:

Write a poem in the form of a letter. To your childhood self? To your future self? To someone you cannot speak to. To an object you appreciate.

(For odes on objects, see Neruda.)

*

What is a survivable routine? By this, I mean, what is a manageable routine, one that will ensure continual production? How does one turn a well into a watermill?

Could I be the water wheel? Sometimes I think I'd like to be the house beside it. They're always so sweet—cobblestoned or Tutor style, glassy water beside it. Sometimes The Quiet is not so terrifying.

*

It is near-night—the gloaming, that time between light—and it's raining. This is my favorite time of year, when the thunderstorms roll across the prairie. Our grass is so tangly-rich, fat with dandelion fluff. Our yard is slick, deep, and dark. Tomorrow, there will be loam. Our compost pile will need turning. I will find something there.

Ars Poetica Schmetica

Amy MacLennan

It's the way you sneak up on language,
clobber it on the head, chuck it to the ground.
Or stake out the metaphor at one a.m.
and knock it over like a corner 7-Eleven.
If you're feeling grounded you can go
with hard, mark, barb
as you follow dear Mr. Hugo
and pull the trigger on the sound in beats
three to eight later.
You would pull piano wire
around your own neck when you poke,
tease, threaten, cajole
any verb to make that line snap.
Beg one feral poem,
all skittish and hissing,
from under the house,
promise clean water, a nice can of tuna
if it would come out,
sniff a bit at your hand,
and just think for a minute
about jumping into your arms.
How you wait and pray for *image*.
How you think *compress*.
Then smear blue ink on your sheets,
fingers, best pants, scratch out
the words on the page to try again.

Little Magazines
John Laue

I tried the Crippled Crab,
The Pomp and Circumstance Review,
Pink Lace Pentagram,
Druid's Phlegm,
Poetry Minutia,
The Nuremburg Rebuttal,
Slam-Dunk Journal,
and the Big Cock Quarterly.

Finally
my poem found a home
in the Galapagos Goose
published by the Catgut Press
and sold on the paths
of Lower Patagonia.

Another credit
added to my tiny list—
but wait:
they say I must subscribe
or they won't print it.

Biting my lip
I write them a check
for $25.00
and seal the envelope
with an authentic
poet's-blood kiss.

An Unknown Poet's Manifesto

John Laue

I don't have to appeal
to academics, satisfy
smug connoisseurs, educate,
elucidate, discriminate,
disseminate if I don't choose to.

I've little reputation to uphold,
feel no urge to stay the same,
blame, tame, or flame anyone;
frighten, heighten, tighten,
or enlighten; be frantic, antic,
or romantic; organize, synthesize,
sermonize, or prophesize.

My place in the world
seems quite secure:
there's no necessity for me
to be famous, infamous,
notorious, uproarious,
glorious, serious, or furious.

My life's no more at stake
than many other men's,
so I don't need to daze,
craze, amaze, or praise;
strain, feign, explain
or entertain; be prophet,
pundit, patriot, or politician.

I don't have to be a Poet,
didn't have to write this poem
(I don't believe in shoulds).

You didn't have to
read it either,
but I thought you would.

Like

Stephanie Burt

"Like" appears to be the only word in English that is both a preposition and an active verb. This is like that. I like that. It can be a noun, too. Like attracts like.

"I like that squirrel and his idiot dance up the tree. / I like that tree hanging wide a little leftward." These lines by Will Schutt, the Yale Younger Poet for 2013, can be read with "like" as a verb or with "like" as a preposition ("I, like that squirrel and his idiot, dance"), although their sense resolves to favor the verb.

"It's what you like, not what you are like": these first words we hear in the film *High Fidelity* come to us as voice-over, spoken by Rob (John Cusack), the haplessly charming romantic lead. The men in that film, and in Nick Hornby's novel, try to substitute the exercise of taste for the more demanding work of getting to know real human beings.

If I can see what you have "liked," over years, on Facebook, I will learn something—perhaps more than you intended—about what you are like.

The more often I like what you like, the more likely it becomes that you are like, and that you will like, me.

"Under no matter what cultural construction, women and men are more like each other than chalk is like cheese, than ratiocination is like raising, than up is like down, or than 1 is like 0." (Eve Kosofsky Sedgwick, *Tendencies*)

For William Wordsworth, writing in 1800, rhyme, meter and sex (he seems to have had in mind only what we would call heterosexual sex) all derive from "the pleasure which the mind derives from the perception of similitude in dissimilitude. This principle is the great spring of the activity of our minds, and their chief feeder. From this principle the direction of the sexual appetite, and all the passions connected with it, take their origin." (preface to *Lyrical Ballads*)

Simile is to metaphor as allegory to symbol and as "fancy," in Samuel Taylor Coleridge's writings, is to "imagination": only the second has the "esemplastic" (another Coleridgean term) power to create something new.

In arithmetic, two straight lines denote equality: =

Two curvy lines, on the other hand (which are like the equals sign, but not the same as the equal sign) denote similarity, likeness, approximation: ≈

Grammarians call the verb to be (is, are) the *copula*.

Bruce Beasley has a disturbing verse essay called "Is," in which sex and procreation are (perhaps too much) like metaphor, and (perhaps too much) like divine creation, to Beasley's adolescent imagination: the copula is too much like copulation.

Consider an unwritten (so far as I know) but easily drafted essay called "The Queer Simile," in which comparisons using *like* or *as* stand for same-sex and non-procreative sexual pleasure, while metaphor, comparison using the copula, stands for heterosexual intercourse.

Romantic and modernist preferences for metaphor <u>could</u> look, from this angle, like assertions of straight privilege, while the obvious artifice in simile (this is not really that, this ≠ that: it's only like that. this ≈ that) makes it akin to camp, and to drag.

"Like," as adjective, adverb, conjunction, preposition and noun (OED): similar, denoting similarity, from Old English *gelic* and Germanic *galiko, ga* (with) + *liko* (body, or form).

Recent OED supplements add the American colloquial sense in which "like" imputes speech or thought: "She was like X" = "She said X" or "She appeared to be thinking X" or "She looked like she was on the point of saying X."

All actual speech is like (is not quite the same as) what we are thinking, what we meant to say.

"Like," as verb (OED): "to find agreeable or congenial; to feel attracted to or favorably impressed." Also from *liko* (body or form), cognate *lich*, Old and Middle English, "body"; what we like conforms to us, fits our bodies, resembles something in us, or else gives our desires right form.

So poetry replaces the body (*liko*) with something whose form (*liko*) is like it, though not identical to it: more vulnerable, or less subject to decay, or harder to read, or easier to read, or more attractive (more likeable) than what we already have.

Frank Bidart has written, so far as I know, the only poem entitled simply "Like." It addresses someone who has guiltily taken a new lover: the new lover who is like, but is not—has replaced, and can never re-place—the former lover, now deceased. "Woe is blunted not erased/ by *like*," Bidart's "Like" begins; "The dead hate *like*, bitter/ when the living with too-small/ grief replace them."

Bidart's ideas echo Freud's "Mourning and Melancholia." His poem uses almost no concrete nouns, as if images, sensory details, representa-tions, belonged to the living alone. To say "like," to be able to say "like," in Bidart's poem is to acknowledge that the dead are not the living, that one lover is not another, that we cannot make this year, or this pleasure, or this commitment, identical to the last, and yet that to live on is to make new commitments anyway, to set them beside (but not in the same place as) the old.

In languages, such as Hebrew and Chinese, that routinely omit the verb "to be," juxtaposition can imply identity. (Thus italics on *is, are and* be in some English Bibles: the Hebrew original lacked the verb.)

In English, though, if something *is* something else, you have to say so: poets can thus imply likeness without even pretending to make an identity, simply by planting noun phrases side by side.

"Like" also serves contemporary speakers—especially young ones—as what linguists call a hesitation form: it is what (or many of us, or perhaps our students, or our children) say when we need more time to articulate, like, what we meant. "Like" serves meanwhile to keep the con-versation going, while saying "I'm speaking; I'm here."

For the literary critic Robert Langbaum, writing in 1959, the kind of poem called dramatic monologue established the mere presence, the fictive existence, of the character it created: its speaker said, in effect, "I exist; I'm here."

In Paul Muldoon's sonnet "Twice," from *The Annals of Chile* (1994), key words repeat (though not in rhyming position), water turns into ice (the same, but not the same), the ice into a mirror (which shows us ourselves, but reversed), and a schoolboy runs from one side of a long-exposure photograph to the other, so that he shows up in the same picture "two places at once, or was it one place twice?" That schoolboy also bears the nickname "'Lefty,' or 'An ciotach,'" which is Irish for "Lefty": the same meaning, not the same word.

In Muldoon's long poem "Yarrow," also from *The Annals of Chile*, "like" appears repeatedly both as preposition and as hesitation form, where it suggests both the self-destructive heroine's forced, awkward youthfulness and the poet's failure to capture her, quite: "the projector had gone, like,/ totally out of frame."

*

The psychoanalyst D.W. Winnicott, in his studies of children, looked at "transitional objects"—blankets, "lovies," cherished dolls, stuffed animals—that mediate between the child herself and the child's idea of the rest of the world. Transitional objects, which calm children down, alleviate sadness and loneliness, serve some (but not all) the functions of parents and friends, are neither me nor not-me, neither wholly imaginary, nor wholly part of the external world, and it is important that the child not have to say (even to herself) to which space the transitional objects belong.

Poems may all be like these transitional objects; speakers in poems may all be like Powers's Helen, or like Pinocchio, the indubitably constructed, artificial boy who wants to be alive, to be real.

Emily Dickinson to T. W. Higginson: "Are you too deeply occupied to say if my verse is alive?"

The literary readers in *Galatea 2.2*—among them the human Richard, and the nonhuman (but probably conscious) Helen, and several other human beings—discover that literature itself is like firsthand experience, but is not an adequate replacement for it, just as writing books is like, but is not, raising children, and just as one language is no substitute for another. "My books are my children," the childless Richard declares at one point, in Italian; neither he, nor his elderly Italian interlocutor, believes it.

Towards the end of the novel, Helen describes herself as occupying a transitional space between life and nonlife, since she can do nothing but read, hear and see: "It is a hard thing to be dropped down halfway."

In Coleridge's own poetry, according to the critic Susan Wolfson, "like" and "as" flag some unsolvable cognitive problem: simile "dramatizes the effort to find a language adequate to represent what is felt to escape representation," showing how it feels when we try to understand something we cannot understand, as at the end of Coleridge's poem "Constancy to an Ideal Object":

> And art thou nothing? Such thou art, as when
> The woodman winding westward up the glen
> At wintry dawn, wher o'er the sheep-track's maze
> The viewless snow-mist weaves a glist'ning haze,
> Sees full before him, gliding without tread,
> An image with a glory round its head:
> The enamoured rustic worships its fair hues,
>
> Nor knows he makes the shadow he pursues!

We have "like," as we have poetry, because we do not ever wholly possess or understand the object of our love.

We exercise language, strenuously, perhaps winsomely, at the cost of all sorts of embarrassment, amateurishly or with great skill, in order to do something together, something that feels like art, and also like the making of a face. (It's not only Crawford who likened this kind of cosmetic work to the poetic creation of persons: consider Shakespeare's sonnet 83.)

Allen Grossman again: "Poetic reading...is a case of the construction of the countenance, the willing of the presence of a person": when we read a poem *as* a poem, we must make up a person, imagine the presence of a made-up face.

"I believe our best work on earth is in service of likeness. I don't know what to call it—moments of interpenetration? "You're writing, I think, to say how much you want to work for such a cause," writes Lia Purpura, in her book *Rough Likeness*.

How would one work "for" the cause of likeness? By writing poetry, in general; in particular, by making and multiplying similes.

Writer Wanted
Brenda Moguez

WRITER WANTED

JOB DESCRIPTION

Previous Experience

• None is required except a burning desire to weave a tale, confess a secret, and live forever on the page (even if that page is a diary you leave behind for your children). A pinch of madness and determination goes a hell of a long way.

Desired Skills

• Possess excellent communication skills and be able to address delicate subjects, such as:
  o   Plot.
  o   Internal and external conflict.
  o   Writing engaging dialogue that reveals character and moves the story forward.
  o   Show and not tell at the right time.
  o   Tell and not show as needed.
• Have strong organizational skills and be a magical problem solver
  o   Keep the facts straight: ages, times of day, places, etc.
  o   Create scenes out of thin air.
  o   Name the characters *correctly*...i.e., Gladys could never have pulled off Scarlett.
  o   Change the tense and point of view after typing THE END.
• Be willing to work variable hours including:
  o   The middle of the day, before coffee (but not recommended), and even at 3 a.m.
  o   Evenings and weekends.
  o   During dinner parties (might include running to the facilities to make a note on a phone app, back of hand, or paper towel).
  o   Daydream when it hits, including mid conversation with

your significant other and when the police officer is writing
you a ticket for talking to yourself in a public setting.

o   Be on standby if the muse visits, an idea settles in, or you
wake up with a story pulsing through your veins.

o   Write—DAILY (This may include work on a Works in
Progress, Dear Diary, memoir entries, morning pages, raw
writing, love letters, or notes on the back of napkins.)

o Write when you'd rather meet your lover (OK, exceptions
are allowed. Lovers should come first; same applies
to children—the small ones. Over 13s can be taught to
respect a crazed writer in the thralls of a creative frenzy.)

Desired Traits

- Extreme quirkiness.
- Willingness to take risks and try new ideas.
- Having a whimsical attitude is a huge plus, as well as the
ability to laugh when tears are more appropriate.
- Deeply passionate.
- Exceptionally forgiving.
- Gritty resolve.
- Gumption.

Requirements:

- Love words.
- Accept writing is a lifetime commitment.
- Respond to the voices in your head in a timely manner.
- Be capable of industrial strength clean-up during editing
phases—must be fearless with the DELETE key.
- There is no *get out of jail free* card (Once you don the
writer persona you are labeled forever more. Even if you
have plastic surgery, change your name, or try to enter the
Witness Protection Program, your voices and your muse
will follow you all the way to Timbuktu.).
- Xena/Hulk-like body and emotional armor REQUIRED

to withstand rejection after rejection.

- Have unlimited faith in yourself (You'll need it.).
- Ability to take constructive criticism without reverting to a fetal position.
- Same Xena/Hulk-like strength required to push past the criticism and self-doubt.
- Comfortable being alone for extended periods of time.
- Strong support network.
- Must assume accountability for quality of the final output.
- Must have a surplus of medical supplies, chocolate chip cookies, and wine.
- Commitment to continuously feed the creative beast— entails long walks, daydreaming, leafing through the magazines, reading the *National Enquirer*, reading books (all kinds), going to museums, listening to music, making lists, taking pictures, breathing, allowing life to flow freely through you...

Benefits and Compensation

- There is no compensation unless you pen the next big thing. Think outside of Bella and Edward, or sex in chains. Dance with the wind.
- Perks—there are none, but if you are still reading, then you're mad as a hatter and deserve to know the rest).
- There is no advancement—NONE AT ALL. Fame and fortune are not the end game.
- Writing is a calling, not a choice. Even the famous and very rich writers accept this about the job.
- Other than sparse to non-existent opportunities for personal growth there isn't any. If, however, you are fearless and don't care about benefits, you might find a passion that will weather all the seasons of your life.

Only apply if you are prepared to go the distance.

Damn the Apostrophe
Amy Rutten

I hesitate when people ask what I do. Depending on who is asking, I may say I'm a licensed architect, a part-time librarian, or that I run a vacation rental business. But what I really want to say is that I'm a writer.

As long as you are writing, successful authors urge, you should call yourself a writer. But even though I dedicate two full days a week to the craft and wake daily at 5:15 a.m. for a few more hours at the keyboard, I'm still reluctant to claim the title. I feel that I need permission, some sort of external validation, a paycheck or a published piece, in order to call myself a writer.

Luckily, I stumbled across another marker recently; one that seems to have nearly as much credibility.

I often start out free writing in the same document every morning. On the advice of Natalie Goldberg, I sit my butt down in my red writing chair in the dark, quiet hours of the morning, my coffee at my side, and attempt to ride bareback through my mind just as dawn is breaking across the page. Don't stop, I tell myself. Don't worry about spelling or grammar. Write into the hard places, the scary places, the places where the energy is. I trip over my own fingers, if I'm doing it right, trying to get the words out before they gallop away from me. That process seems to work, but the document itself is awash in a sea of red and blue: Microsoft Word's underline of shame under every misspelling, run-on sentence, fragment, incorrect punctuation, and broken grammatical rule. But it is in this document that almost every decent thing I've ever written has been born. I have named this document Zen Mind, and, frankly, it's a mess.

But last Thursday morning, at 5:17 a.m., my view of those pages changed. I sat in my red chair, fire in the hearth, writing furiously on page 357 of that single spaced 220,000-word document when a message popped up on my screen:

There are too many grammatical and spelling errors to continue displaying them in this document. Spelling and Grammar notification will now be shut off.

I was mortified.

Like most writers, I write with my inner critic perched on my shoulder, whispering in my ear, pointing out why I have no right to say what I am saying, to feel what I am feeling, to commit my energy to the endeavor of writing when I obviously have no talent. I have spent too much time listening to that critic. Sometimes it causes me to second-guess my words. Some days I have let it talk me out of writing altogether. Years ago, I let it talk me into committing heinous crimes, like getting a degree in architecture. Was this it? The external message I had been waiting for? The proof that I truly *was* a terrible writer?

But there was one part of me, albeit a small part, that refused to believe it. That part of me looked at the message this way:

What if Microsoft Word's Spellcheck is just a digital manifestation of my inner critic? I knew from my experience in this very document that the best writing, my best writing, is the writing that is so filled with energy neither the writing nor the energy can be contained on the page. Every painter knows that a painting is not about the subject, it's about capturing light on a flat canvas. And every real writer knows that it does not matter how you write, as long as you are capturing the energy of your thoughts on the page. That is the kind of energy that leaps right into the reader and makes a connection, the kind of energy that can spark a fire or start a revolution. The kind of energy that cannot be diagrammed in a sentence.

So what if someone at Microsoft arbitrarily decided that after 1,000 mistakes, or 10,000 mistakes, it's no longer worth pointing out the errors? Maybe there is some limit to mistakes, and maybe I reached it, but what if there was one programmer who realized that anyone showing up to the same document day after day, mistakes and all, might not be striving for perfect grammar? Maybe that programmer imagined a writer donning his or her armor (a pen or a keyboard, a cup of coffee or a cigarette) and going to battle with their inner critic, fighting to get each word down on the page before it scrambled off to hide in some corner, having been terrified into submission by the Grammar Police? And what if this programmer thought: *You know what? If you are going to write long enough and hard enough to make 10,000 mistakes, then we here at Microsoft are just going to give you a hall pass to do whatever you want with the rest of this document. You've got it under control. You've won. No more critic. Be free and write, my friend. Hats off to you.*

I heard that small voice clearly as I silently fist pumped in my red chair last Thursday morning. That's what I chose to believe. A free pass. I did it. I showed up to the page nearly every day for four years. I made mistake after mistake after mistake. I've made mistakes every day since Thursday. But now, no one cares. Not Microsoft, not me. I've transcended my own inner critic. Stuck a pencil in its eye and heard it yell 'uncle' as it fell to the floor beside my chair.

Damn the apostrophe, fuck the capital letter, and to hell with the incorrect use of *their*. Just let me write. Why?

Because I'm a writer.

Why I Write

E. Ce Miller

I am curious.

Famous last words that doomed the cat and probably several dozen sea-faring Greek myths over the years and yet…well, that's where it all starts, isn't it? I am curious. Curiosity is the thing that propels me to think: this will make a great story—a simple idea and yet within it resides the impetus for my whole life. I write because I am painfully and inconveniently and unavoidably curious.

I have no idea what writing should be—and I'm not sure that's the kind of thing that interests me. What I know is what I love—the way a really great story can somehow braid itself into the narrative of my life. I know that when Dalton Trumbo's Joe picked up his gun and hopelessly marched off to make the world safe for the myth of democracy, my heart forever broke for Kareen, who he left at home. I know that decades after he lost Julia to the Establishment, George Orwell compelled me to peer into the corners of my bedroom, searching for hidden cameras. I know that every time Allen Ginsberg wailed "I'm with you in Rockland," my life changed just a little bit more.

I write because when Janis Joplin went down the river Jordan and when Jefferson Airplane broke through the sound barrier and when Grace Slick followed the White Rabbit down, down, down for no other reason than to find Alice and ask her a question, I wanted to go too. I write because in 1969 Wavy Gravy hosted breakfast in bed for 400,000 and I missed it. I write because when I knelt on the sidewalk at Kent State with Crosby, Stills, Nash and Young, I was thirty years too late. I write because Jim Morrison told me to "Break on through…" and writing is the only way I know how.

The authors I started reading: Trumbo, Orwell, Ginsberg; and Hunter Thompson, Joan Didion, and Norman Mailer—they showed me what it was I wanted to be. But the music…the music is what taught me how to get there. Those imperfect, pre-auto tune, throaty voices wailing poetry through the peeling foam of my hand-me-down MK Goliath speakers taught me about the power—and the danger— of words. The musicians of the 1960s and 70s were scrappy. They weren't afraid to say anything. They were curious and they weren't afraid to push that curiosity to the absolute last remaining limitation. They were rowdy and combative, and they challenged the status quo. Their words took me on journeys across the world and across the universe and deep into myself. They believed that their music had the capacity to change the world, and through their poetry they assembled a merry band of followers who believed along with them. They were the rallying cries playing softly in the background when I put pen to paper and began scratching out all the things that I wanted to say. Through music, I learned not only to physically see the poetry—the visual quality of one letter curving into another—but to *hear* it as well; to listen to the sound of the words aloud, to stand in the middle of that noise, to carry the words along with me and to play them over and over in my mind until they became as close to exactly right as possible.

I love lines that begin with the word "Furthermore." I love writers who aren't afraid to use nine semi-colons in the same sentence. I think more novels should end in italics. I admire writers who invent their own words. I don't think twenty-six letters are enough. I think we're too preoccupied with the distinctions between fact and truth. I think stories are owned by their characters. I think characters teach writers how to tell their stories.

The stories I love are the stories abundant with possibility; stories through which I can reclaim lost loves, catch flights left unboarded, rent apartments in cities far from home, respond to questions I'd refused to answer, befriend characters once feared. The stories I love are the stories that have a sense of justice to them; a redemptive quality; the stories that manage to correct that which real life got wrong. I love stories that amend past mistakes, stories that avert disaster and rescue those characters left neglected by the facts of history. I love writing that lets me choose differently.

I love writing that is composed with great love, great intention and great intensity; writing that is written because it is unavoidable, because one has created something good and beautiful and important and it must be put out into the world. I write because of an unwavering conviction that when the money is gone and the grid has crashed and there's no more oil and the well is dry, those left standing will be the artists.

Manifesto

Megan Jeanine Tilley

- Three books can fit in my purse. I picked it out for that specifically. I read them on my lunch break. I've read the spines off of at least twenty. I keep them in their own box because I feel too bad throwing them away.

- After a particularly nasty call with an insurance company, I will sit and work on any number of short stories saved on my desktop under names like "Yearly Audit" and "Memo #4". This is my last year applying to MFA programs. I'm afraid all my documents will stay saved under corporate sounding names, so I work harder. Fear is okay. Stopping because of fear is not okay.

- Red wine should be bought in big bottles, and it's okay if I drink them out of old pasta sauce jars because I haven't emptied the dishwasher because I've been drafting and editing, and that is important.

- I am the poltergeist of local used bookstores. I buy books I know I *should* read—Chekhov, Faulkner, Capote, O'Connor, Hemingway— and allow myself two fantasy books per trip. I keep a notebook of quotes. That's important so I can keep them in check.

- It's okay if pages end up getting deleted. Not everything I write will be good. Most of it will be horrible. Sometimes they'll be *really horrible*, and I'll climb into bed and pretend that I never wrote. As long as the next day I try again, it's okay to sulk.

- Indulge in genre fiction. Write genre fiction. Write about bogans and sidhe and dragons in the subway system of New York City. But don't get lost—learn from both sides. Both sides are important. My first love doesn't have to be my only.

- Learn from others. Learn from everyone. Everyone has something to offer.

Where Stories Come From

Laura Steadham Smith

I write because I might be the worst person I know. I write because azaleas bloom in spring. I write to remember what it felt like to run through the woods as a kid. I write to become someone else. I write because one of my favorite sounds is pride in my Dad's voice. I write because other people are infinitely more interesting than I am. I write because I am too many different people to keep track of.

I write because I over-think everything. I write because I'm a narcissist. I write because I hate myself. I write because I'm not good at talking. I write because counseling costs money and booze is bad for my liver. I write because I think that, maybe someday, I'll figure things out. I write because I'm lonely. I write because of Laura Ingalls Wilder. I write because I don't want to admit I wish I had gone to med school. I write because I have to. I write because I'm too type A to function and need a place for my thoughts to go after I've organized all the dishes in matching pairs and made to-do lists of all the clutter inside my head. I write because sometimes music takes too much energy.

I write because sometimes I want to. I write to say something beautiful. I write because I want other people to understand each other. I write because I don't understand anyone. I write because knowing thyself seems like a good idea. I write because I think empathy is the most important virtue in the world. I write because I'm too selfish to be empathetic.

I write because I like words—their rhythm, their melody, the way they fill a space with sound and light. I write because the world is connected. I write because people are all the same. I write because people make no sense and are totally different. I write because I want someone to listen to me. I write because I found myself in books. I write because I read so much as a kid that I have weak social skills and making friends is hard. I write because sometimes finding a quiet hillside to watch leaves fall and read about other people's lives becomes lonely.

I write because good people do terrible things. I write because I like making people laugh. I write because I cry when I see kindness and I'm not supposed to feel things that deeply. I write because I like drinking coffee and staring out the window. I write to prove to myself that I'm not lazy or spoiled. I write because I might not be lazy, but I'm definitely spoiled. I write because color and imagery glitter and I like shiny things. I write because magic.

I write because my grandfather built his own house, and I want someone to remember. I write because my grandmother carried demons until she died and passed them on to her children. I write to exorcise them, and I hide my stories from my family. I write because my story is one of many. I write because sometimes red clay roads lead to warm fireplaces and fried catfish and happy dogs. I write because sometimes wraparound porches hide bodies.

I write because everyone loves to hate rednecks. I write because I do, too, but I am ashamed when I meet people with dirt under their fingernails because I know I don't work that hard. I write because I'm angry. I write because I'm hopeful. I write because I don't know how to change my own oil or drive a four-wheeler—only how to hold onto the back without falling off. I write because I'm a glutton for punishment. I write because an ex-boyfriend told me writing made me brave.

I write because I spend less time on GChat these days. I write because I'm manipulative and hypocritical. I write because I've been doing it so long I think I have to. I write because I like telling stories. I write to play pretend as a grownup. I write because nothing about me feels very grown up—not my stack of self-obsessed journals or the receipts stuffed in my desk drawer or the scuffed shoes under my bed, the ones I used to wear to punk shows.

I write because I'm crazy enough to believe I could tell you something about yourself.

Navels Are Natural

Caroll Sun Yang

Do you, you feel like I do?
Do you, you feel like I do?
-Peter Frampton

Being an artist is like being a wrung-out rag, making and mopping up messes, bunched up in the corner, oft hung to dry, wearing history on our sleeves, smelling of our own mammal ripeness and occasionally being thrown in with the real wash. We who soak in alphabets, images, and sounds know that all arts demand that we uphold a fundamental oath to act as shaman, seers, provocateurs, *enfants terrible*, politicians, romancers, therapists, charmers, jokesters, witches, pioneers, maniacs, hookers…and all of this sexily, to boot. If we fail at these tasks—oh arduous hours flecked with blessed golden play—then our lives will seem utterly wasted. Our creative callings failed. Leaks in the hot tin roofs. Ancient toilets stopped up. Lives less lived. Muzzled. We are about to blow!

If I seem melodramatic and insecure, it is because I am. In this lowly state, I let my mind wander off to pasture. Chewing the cud, metaphorical green juice dribbling down my shirtfront, prostrate in bed, covered in ancient fawn quilting à la thrift store, cats fighting at my feet like warm lumps of tangling frisk. My gut consists of Mr. Pibb carbonation dancing with a cheap chile relleno burrito all laced with psychotropics. I burn. I feel strong. Full of jitterbugging ideas jostling into place. Visions. Sounds. Alphabets. Maybe my aura is now lava.

I am typing on a cellular QWERTY pad and words tumble after one another on an eerily lit screen sized smaller than a maxi-pad (great metaphors abound), my skull and brain, propped up on two pillows, growing heavier with each word, double chin at attention, heartbeat slowing to a meditative rate, legs like dumb sticks. My life has been reduced to thumb typing essays on the same devices that boisterous *MTV* and Tyra Banks reality show participants showily make use of. Their devices announce: "Meet at the holy hell wrecking ball platform wearing sneakers and bath-

ing suits at 8 a.m.! Get ready for a raunchy, mad blast! Today is elimina-
tion day." Or "Be fierce! Today you will walk the runway for anonymous
couture designer, winner will be treated to anonymous jeweler's jewels
and full body massages!" My humble cell announces no such sport. At 8
a.m. I am usually shuttling children to school, teeth unclean, sunglasses
hiding yesterday's raccoon eyes, donning paint splattered tee and torn
pajama bottoms, breasts swinging free, naked feet, throttling through
the drive-through Starbucks. My text messages read like, "Where r u?" to
which I might respond with, "Ded." Or on a decent day, "Writing. xo."
I run with a pack that the uninitiated might describe as "lazy good-for-
nothings." We artists do not pace in straight sober lines, solving problems like accountants, optometrists or soldiers. We professional imagin-
ers pace the ground raw in drunken lines, darting in and out of reality,
occasionally leaping from the sheer thrill of "breaking through." We in-
ventors, theorists, artists, writers, musicians...struggle, but in the name
of what exactly? Exactly.

We are generally benign, somewhat opinionated, obsessive nerds.
While the universe propels forward, infinite events occurring simultaneously, we feel caught in its sway. It is our job to mark time/space in
unique ways while attempting to engage others. Sometimes we will fail
at this; many hours will be lost to intense examinations of life, but some
hours we will make magic- magnificently warping perceptions. On days
when I feel especially wrung out, halted and alone- I seek out my fatherly
path pavers. Dear Mr. Italo Calvino, I sit in this first world abode, re-
clined in a puffy chair, jacked up on fair trade coffee. I gulp your enchant-
ing words. I succumb to waves of nausea, the general turbulence of a gut
trying to survive while immersed in the daily task of "making meaning."
I look for my mirror image in your stories and am overtaken by jealousy
at your skill, a jealousy intersected by admiration and understanding:

> *Work stops at sunset. Darkness falls over the building site. The sky is filled*
> *with stars. "There is the blueprint," they say.*

But somewhere, someone less fortunate than I (sitting on a cold,
hard curb drinking homeless "mission" tap water) is sharing a not glam-
orous sandwich with someone less fortunate than they (an under-com-

pensated, discarded and limbless war veteran) and they commune with teary eyes of gratitude.

My dizzy companion Roland Barthes, in "A Lover's Discourse," you treat me with your text. Curled up fetal on an inflatable mattress, fighting the spins, I read the same opening sentence over and over again during my first and last heroin high:

> *I am engulfed, I succumb…Outburst of annihilation which affects the amorous subject in despair or fulfillment.*

Simultaneously, a prehistoric species of a never before seen deep-sea creature, a blind gelatinous angel embedded with blinking lights, is being drug up in a fishing net. It is briefly studied, announced on the world news and promptly dies in captivity.

Darling F. Scott Fitzgerald, your stories I recite aloud to myself, channeling fictional characters in front of the mirror the way only high school girls and gay men do best, sporting brick red lipstick and hot-ironed ringlets, Kiss-Me-Kismine for the day:

> *I never noticed the stars before. I always thought of them as great big diamonds that belonged to someone. Now they frighten me. They make me feel that it was all a dream, all my youth.*

Meanwhile, my less neurotic peers are prancing in the California sunshine, cheering for teams, sharing malts, and making good old-fashioned time. In such glorious health.

Magnificent "Books of Art I, II, III": when the salesman comes to the door and persuades mother to purchase you as a set, it's the best $200 she will ever spend. I am saved. From the first moment I crack you open, I set off a chain of longing. Hours spent pining for naked people… reposed in overgrown gardens, drowning in apocalyptic storms with orgiastic bodies, tossed by waves. I sleep on checkered floors in moody parlors, conquer brightly pigmented villages, lose my mind in geometric demonstrations, and befriend forlorn saloon maids. You all stoke my fires. Obsessed from the start. This very second, countless slippery wailing newborns are being severed at the cord.

Gasp. I once made a friend in a 72-hour holding facility. He and I were 5150's, an impersonal numerical designation for those needing an "Involuntary Psychiatric Hold." He showed me his feet, blistered from too much walking without destination. His body cracked-out, delirious with hunger pains that I have never known. His true love left him, driving him raving mad, so that every single woman he meets is merely a "shadow of her shadow." I know shadows of shadows, I have been a shadow, and I have been a shadow's shadow. *Shadow* is a beautiful word. I asked him if he thought so too. He said yes, lit fires in his eyes, then fell promptly in love with me. He shared that none had ever been so kind to him without expecting a return favor. It pleased me to hear this. So I ceremoniously slipped off my black patent leather ballet flats (with pre-coital flare) and I showed him my feet. *Princess this.* Even he cringed.

My feet are calloused and picked, bloody scabs in spots where the skin was torn too far and deep. My own hands wreak this mess. A nervous habit, perhaps of someone whose life is spent in too much reverie with fingers idle. Nervous hands in need of occupation when not propping up chins, scratching temples, serving diners, tending children, writing words, painting worlds, holding hands…We silently put our shoes back on, unwilling to unpack the stories held there. Instead, this sand-blown, ultraviolet-eyed, hard-living nomad discussed with me the cultural/personal significance of various Led Zeppelin songs. We smoked cigarettes doled by white-robed attendants, while standing in a barren courtyard surrounded by high brick walls. A lone potted fern marking center. A leaking basketball without a hoop. All beat by the sun. We beautifully elaborated the emotional and sonic qualities of the song "Over the Hills and Far Away," its suitability to being heard over tear-tainted beers, between star-crossed lovers, these lines an artist's anthem:

> *Many times I've lied—Many times I've listened*
> *Many times I've wondered how much there is to know.*

Why aren't there music, art and text libraries in psychiatric wards? Upon my release, he gave me the number to his mother's home. He planned to return to her. Exiled from everywhere. We swore to stay in touch. I never called him but I did save the piece of paper with his digits scrawled on it, buried it in my hope-for-nothing chest; I want to unearth it when it comes time to search for my youth, when no more new stories can be lived. I think about our feet sometimes. How they told different stories. Ailed in secret ways. Deeply transcending their primary function as stabilizing agents. What about Auguste Rodin's "The Thinker?" Surely his feet resembled ours, a maze of dry rivulets collecting dirt and battle wounds from places been, skin packed down with years, worn from pacing, ragged with pondering, wise with wandering. If only we were all such heroic figures.

On rare brave occasions, I am my own hero. Like the time I presented an object in art school, a black velvet display case (normally reserved for entomological specimens) which housed pieces of skin peeled from my feet, pinned down with identification tags noting where the dermal bits were abandoned: under the dining table, behind the headboard, in my pea coat pocket, at ex's house, in the dogs mouth, floating at the top of the fish tank...each one accompanied by a brief explanation (a girl can be a creep in such secret and affective ways). The only comment made in the critique was by a mealy-mouthed, anemic boy daintily eating a dry toasted bagel, "Well, I am having a hard time negotiating this bagel and your skin." So I bared a little tooth and giggled, leaned forward with suggestiveness, my fingers laced, drawling in an old tyme barmaid's accent, "Son, maybe you just need a tall drink." The entire room exhaled. There was laughter. Some odd joy in me. That was all that needed to be said. It's all just hunger. We are hungry. Too natural for words. Listen, I got things to launder. Fathers to make. Scenes to brew. Navels to gaze. Questions to formulate. Mistakes to make. Beauty to seek. Galaxies to sort. All kinds of mammal sexy to be. Over the hills and far away waits. I think I *will* get out of bed.

Wrighting Rules and Notes
Jeff Fearnside

Wrules of Righting

1. Play with the language. Stretch it, pull it like taffy, throw it around the room and see where it sticks. Pull it off the wall and examine the stain. Use that too. Have fun.

2. Be human. Don't become too "literary." Live my life fully in all its aspects—physical, mental, emotional, sexual/creative, and spiritual—and write as I live my life.

3. Don't think too much. Write as daringly, openly, sloppily as possible, and clean up the mess (edit) later.

4. Write with intention, purpose, and reverence, but remember: this is creation. It will explode in my head and render all my intentions useless.

5. Unless I speak with my own voice, creation is lost—it's then imitation. Speak with my own voice!

6. Go with the flow. Don't force the material. If the material becomes stuck, don't give up: take a break, do some push-ups, dance to music. But always go back to the writing. No one is forcing me to do this; it's my free and conscious choice.

7. Finish my projects!

Notes to Self When Writing

A writer must stand fearless before the truth, listen carefully, and report it accurately.

Having an outline is good, it provides a place to start from, but always pay more attention to the characters and story as they develop than to my preconceived notions of what they should be. Follow their leads. Take risks.

Write like my favorite jazz players play my favorite jazz, with equal parts artistry and passion, creating a mood but also providing spiritual substance, a fusion of different elements (styles, cultures) true to all and slave to none—something new, alive, and relevant.

Have fun. Break every rule. Let it rip! *Anything.* Sort it out later. It's not a waste of time. I have time. Let the original breath of God, reeking with the interstellar garlic, leeks, and blood-red wine of the Big Bang, breathe through me. Dig, dig into the soil of my imagination. Go to where the Wild Things are. Whatever small portion of genius may have been allotted to me, touch it. Embrace it. Poetry, magical incantations, journalistic reports, simple lists—use them, embrace them all. Remain open to possibility. And try not to be so damn serious all the time!

Don't even think about whether my writing is too popular or too literary, not popular or not literary enough. Just write. Others will decide how to categorize it.

It's important to note that it wasn't always fashionable, especially in other cultures, even today, to be so neutral in writing—to avoid politics, religion, and philosophy. Go ahead: take a stance on something. The trick is not to be pedantic.

Immediate, cut-to-the-bone language. Elegant language. Rich, full language. Wide and expansive. Nuanced and shadowed. Why limit myself for the sake of Emerson's hobgoblin consistency? Don't be afraid to play with my full complement of tools. Don't be afraid to linger on an image or idea, but don't let the story lag, either!

The lively, condensed language of poetry, the narrative drive of a short story, with prudent colorings of philosophy, religion, politics, science, history, natural history (landscape as character)—don't be afraid to *use all my tools!*

While I prefer Emerson's language of light, Denis Johnson's reality—that is, a description of our ignorance of who we are—can provide an effective contrast. Use all my tools. Don't become slave to anyone's writing dogma, least of all my own.

Collage and Appropriation
David Shields

Origin Myth #1

I'm not a big believer in Major Epiphanies, especially those that occur in the shower, but I had one, and it occurred in the shower. Working on *Handbook for Drowning: A Novel in Stories*, I had the sudden intuition that I could take various fragments of things—aborted stories, out-takes from novels, journal entries, lit-crit—and build a story out of them. I really had no idea what the story would be about; I just knew I needed to see what it would look like to set certain shards in juxtaposition with other shards.

Now I have trouble working any other way, but I can't emphasize enough how strange it felt at the time, working in this modal mode. The initial hurdle (and much the most important one) was being willing to follow this inchoate intuition, yield to the prompting, not fight it off, not retreat to the tried-and-true. I thought the story probably had something to do with obsession; I wonder where I got that idea—rummaging through boxes of old papers, riffling through drawers and computer files, crawling around on my hands and knees on the living room floor, looking for bits and pieces I thought might cohere if I could just join them together.

Scissoring and taping together paragraphs from previous projects, moving them around in endless combinations, completely rewriting some sections, jettisoning others, I found a clipped, hard-bitten tone entering the pieces. My work had never been sweet, but this seemed harsher, sharper, even a little hysterical. That tone is, in a sense, the plot of the story: by the end, the reader, feeling, I hope, the depth of my main character's solipsism, understands why the close-third-person narration is so acerbic. Antonya Nelson once said to me that she thought in any work that comes together, the writer had to get lucky, by which I took her to mean that at least one more drawer of meaning has to open up beneath the drawer you, the writer, thought you were opening. I thought

I was writing a story about obsession. I was really writing a story about the hell of obsessive ego.

It really was pretty revelatory and exciting for me to see how part of something I had originally written as an essay about James Joyce's "The Dead" could now be turned sideways and used as the final, bruising insight into my alter ego's psyche. All literary possibilities opened up for me with this story. The way my mind thinks—everything is connected to everything else—suddenly seemed transportable into my writing. I could play all the roles I want to play (reporter, fantasist, autobiographer, essayist, critic). I could call on my strengths (meditation and analysis), hide my weaknesses (plot and plot), be as smart on the page as I wanted to be. I'd found a way to write that seemed true to how I am in the world.

Origin Myth #2

Asked how he came to write so seamlessly about the intersection of personal and political lives, Milan Kundera said it's not hard when you go to the grocery store and the cannon of a Soviet tank is wedged into the back window. When I read Kundera's statement (and wondered what if anything was the American equivalent of the Soviet tank), I was thirty years old, unemployed, broke, lying on my father's couch in an apartment in San Francisco, and watching a performer on TV pretend to be having trouble juggling knives while riding a unicycle. Actually, he was in exquisite control of both the unicycle and the knives; I loved how he pretended not to be. I even started crying, and I realized that part of what moved me to tears was that I was watching this on TV—this was one more level of distance and control—and that if I had been watching him live, I almost certainly wouldn't have been moved anywhere nearly as much, i.e., the degree of removal was central to my emotional engagement with the scene. Which to me was the answer to Kundera's Soviet tank: the American equivalent is the ubiquity of the camera, the immense power of the camera lens on our lives, on my life, on the way I think about life.

I resolved to write a novel (my fourth) about this, and my model was

Kundera's own *The Unbearable Lightness of Being*, in which romantic love was the prism through which the dominant mythology of the culture—in his case, the kitsch of Communism—gets examined. I wanted to do something similar with a married couple and American media/celebrity culture. I took notes on thousands of color-coded 3 x 5 cards. I read innumerable books by cultural critics, from Theodor Adorno to Marc Crispin Miller. I wrote many meditations and reportorial riffs, which I thought I would incorporate into my novel as Kundera incorporated his digressions (in truth, the only parts of his book that engaged me). I watched a staggering number of movies and TV shows, trying to chart my reactions even as I was having them. And try though I might for many, many years—almost my entire thirties—I couldn't work up the requisite interest in the warfare between the husband and wife or boyfriend and girlfriend. I didn't believe in it, since my wife's and my takes weren't vastly dissimilar, and any staged debate seemed very staged, very debatable. I couldn't bring myself to give the two "characters" jobs, such as high school English teacher and film critic for a provincial newspaper. I knew what our jobs were, and they weren't fascinating fodder for fiction. I wasn't interested in imaginary beings' friction vis à vis mass culture; I was interested in my own ambivalence toward mass culture.

My own failure of imagination? Sure, but as Virginia Woolf said in a passage that I reread hundreds of times the fall of 1991, "The test of a book (to a writer) is if it makes a space in which, quite naturally, you can say what you want to say. This proves that a book is alive: because it has not crushed anything I wanted to say, but allowed me to slip it in, without any compression or alteration." The novel for me was nothing but compression and crushing alteration. Desperate, I thought of asking a former student if I could use some passages she'd written—as ballast for a ship I couldn't get out to sea. When I thought I would never be able to write anything again, my daughter Natalie was born and the physical universe suddenly seemed unforgivably real. I newly knew that the digressions were the book. The seeming digressions were all connected. The book was everything in front of me. The world is everything that is the case.

This book became *Remote: Reflections on Life in the Shadow of Celebrity,* which was my Natalie-down-the-rabbit-hole moment. I've never touched terra infirma again. Everything I've written since has been collage (from the French "coller," "to glue").

By the late '90s, my early forties, I'd stopped writing or reading much if any fiction. I was weary unto death of teaching fiction writing. I would teach standardly great stories, and I would admire them from afar, and sometimes students would love the stories, but I had no real passion anymore for, say, Joyce's "The Dead." I could see what made stories like Joyce's "great" or good or at least well-made, but I had and have zero interest in doing something similar. I was watching a lot of self-reflexive documentary films (e.g., Ross McElwee), reading a lot of anthropological autobiographies (e.g., Renata Adler), listening to a lot of stand-up (e.g., Rick Reynolds) and watching a lot of performance art (e.g., Sandra Bernhard). This was the kind of work that truly excited me, and there was a radical disjunction between the books I was pseudo-espousing in class and the books that I loved reading outside of class and was trying to write on my own. The teaching—the falsity of the teaching—forced me to confront and find and define and refine and extend my own aesthetic. It was thrilling. I once was lost and now am found. (Now I'm lost again, but that's another story, which I'll talk about a little later.)

I felt as if I were taking money under false pretenses, so in order to justify my existence to myself, my colleagues, and my students, I developed a graduate course in the self-reflexive gesture in essay and documentary film. The course reader was an enormous, unwieldy, blue packet of hundreds upon hundreds of statements about nonfiction, literary collage, lyric essay. That packet was my life raft: it was teaching me what it was I was trying to write.

Each year, the packet became less unwieldy, less full of repetitions and typographical errors, contained more of my own writing, and I saw how I could push the statements—by myself and by others—into rubrics or categories. All the material about hip-hop would go into its own chapter. So, too, the material about reality TV, memory, doubt, risk, genre, the reality-based community, brevity, collage, contradiction, doubt, etc. Twenty-six chapters, 618 mini-sections. All *Reality Hunger* ever was to me was that blue life-raft: a manuscript in which I was articulating for myself, my students, my peers, and any potential fellow-travelers who might want to come along for the ride for the aesthetic tradition out of which I was writing. It wasn't the novel. And it wasn't memoir. It was something else. It was the idea that all great works of literature either dissolve a genre or invent one. If you want to write serious books, you must be ready to break the forms. It's a commonplace that every book needs to find its own form, but how many really do? Coetzee on his own work: "Nowhere do you get a feeling of a writer deforming his medium in order to say what has never been said before, which is to me the mark of great writing."

And here was the big break: I realized how perfectly the appropriated and remixed words embodied my argument. Just as I was arguing for work that occupied a bleeding-edge between genres, so, too, I wanted the reader to experience in my mash-up the dubiety of the first-person pronoun. I wanted the reader to not quite be able to tell who was talking— was it me or Sonny Rollins or Emerson or Nietzsche or David Salle or, weirdly, none of us or all of us at the same time?

Until that point, I hadn't thought a great deal about the degree to which the book appropriated and remixed other people's words. It seemed perfectly natural to me. I love the work of a lot of contemporary visual artists whose work is bound up with appropriation—Richard Prince, Sherrie Levine, Cindy Sherman, Elaine Sturtevant, Christian Marclay, Glenn Ligon. And I've been listening to rap since Grandmaster Flash in the late '70s. Why in the world would contemporary writing not be able to keep pace with the other arts?

Most readers of the book-as-intended would have spotted only a handful of the most well-known quotations, suspected that a lot of the paragraphs were quotations (even when they couldn't quite place them), and come to regard my *I* as a floating umbrella self, sheltering simultaneously one voice ("my own") and multiple voices. The possibility that every word in the book might be quotation and not "original" to the author could have arisen. The whole argument of that version of the book was to put "reality" within quadruple quotation marks. Reality isn't straightforward or easily accessible; it's slippery, evasive. Just as authorship is ambiguous, knowledge is dubious, and truth is unknown or, at the very least, relative.

My publisher, Knopf, which is a division of Random House, which is a subset of Bertelsmann, a multinational, multi-billion-dollar corporation, didn't see it the same way. I consulted numerous copyright attorneys, and I wrote many impassioned emails to my editor and the Random House legal department. At one point, I considered withdrawing the book and printing it at Kinko's (now a subset of FedExOffice). Random House and I worked out a compromise whereby there would be no footnotes in the text, but there would be an appendix in the back with citations in very, very small type (if you're over fifty, good luck reading it). Quite a few of the citations are of the "I can't quite remember where this is from" variety. The appendix is prefaced by a disclaimer in which I say, "I'm writing to regain a freedom that writers from Montaigne to Burroughs took for granted and that we have lost," and I urge the reader to "grab a sharp pair of scissors and remove the appendix along the dotted vertical line. Stop. Don't read any farther."

Some people seemed to think I was the anti-Christ because I didn't genuflect at the twin altars of the novel and intellectual property (there's a misnomer if ever there was one). I became, briefly, the poster boy for The Death of the Novel and The End of Copyright. Fine by me. Those have become something close to my positions. The key thing for an intellectually rigorous writer to come to grips with is the marginalization of literature by more technologically sophisticated and thus more visceral forms. You can work within these forms or write about them or through them or appropriate the strategies these forms use, but it's not a very good idea to go on writing in a vacuum. The novel was invented to access interiority. Now, most people communicate through social media, and everyone I know under thirty has remarkably little notion of privacy. The novel is an artifact, which is why antiquarians cling to it so fervently. Art, like science, progresses. Forms evolve. Forms are there to serve the culture, and when they die, they die for a good reason.

Definitions of collage

I love literature, but not because I love stories per se. I find nearly all the moves the traditional novel/memoir makes unbelievably predictable, tired, contrived, and essentially purposeless. I can never remember characters' names, plot developments, lines of dialogue, details of setting. It's not clear to me what such narratives are supposedly revealing about the human condition. I'm drawn to literature instead as a form of thinking, consciousness, wisdom-seeking. I like work that's focused not only page by page but line by line on what the writer really cares about rather than hoping that what the writer cares about will somehow mysteriously creep through the cracks of narrative, which is the way I experience most stories and novels. Collage works are nearly always "about what they're about"—which may sound a tad tautological—but when I read a book that I really love, I experience the excitement that in every paragraph the writer is manifestly exploring his subject.

I'm not interested in collage as the refuge of the compositionally disabled. I'm interested in collage as (to be honest) an evolution beyond narrative.

Conventional fiction/memoir teaches the reader that life is a coherent, fathomable whole that concludes in neatly wrapped-up revelation. Life, though—standing on a street corner, channel surfing, trying to navigate the web or a declining relationship, hearing that a close friend died last night—flies at us in bright splinters. (Lance Olsen)

All definitions of montage share a common denominator; they all imply that meaning is not inherent in any one shot but is created by the juxtaposition of shots. Lev Kuleshov, an early Russian filmmaker, intercut images of an actor's expressionless face with images of a bowl of soup, a woman in a coffin, and a child with a toy. Viewers of the film praised the actor's performance; they saw in his face (emotionless as it was), hunger, grief, and affection. They saw, in other words, what was not really there in the separate images. Meaning and emotion were created not by the content of the individual images but by the relationship of the images to one another. (Vivian Sobchack)

A great painting comes together, just barely. (Picasso)

A mosaic, made out of broken dishes, makes no attempt to hide the fact that it's made out of broken dishes, in fact flaunts it.

Momentum, in literary mosaic, derives not from narrative but the subtle, progressive buildup of thematic resonances.

Any opportunity that a writer has to engage the reader intimately in the act of creating the text is an opportunity to grab onto. White space does that. I don't ever want to be bored, and I certainly don't ever want any of my readers to be bored. I'd much rather risk them getting annoyed and frustrated than bored. (John D'Agata)

Everything I write, I believe instinctively, is to some extent collage. Meaning, ultimately, is a matter of adjacent data.

The very nature of collage demands fragmented materials, or at least materials yanked out of context. Collage is, in a way, only an accentuated act of editing: picking through options and presenting a new arrangement (albeit one that, due to its variegated source material, can't be edited into the smooth, traditional whole that a work of complete fiction could be). The act of editing may be the key postmodern artistic instrument. (Nina Michelson)

In collage, writing is stripped of the pretense of originality and appears as a practice of mediation, of selection and contextualization, a practice, almost, of reading. (Lance Olsen)

Appropriation

I'm not an anti-copyright absolutist; I'm not the director of *The King's Speech* and don't walk around selling DVDs of that film with my name on it. There are three crucial terms when it comes to copyright: fair use—you can quote ten percent or less of a book, or 250 words or fewer from a shorter work; public domain—you can quote from Kipling, since he's been dead for more than seventy-five years; and, most importantly, transformation—in your appropriation of another work, are you simply plagiarizing, or are you remaking it? This is where it gets harder to define and most interesting (immediately after I asked a student if she'd copied a passage from Wikipedia, she changed the Wikipedia entry, erasing the evidence). Lawyers, servants of late-market capitalism, want a bright line now, but in the history of art there has never been a bright line.

A system of writing was invented in isolation (at most) four times. The first system of writing was invented in Mesopotamia. The second might have been in Egypt, but there's a compelling argument that the Mesopotamians influenced the birth of the Egyptian writing system. The third was in China, and again there's debate about whether the Mesopotamians influenced the Chinese. The fourth, and only the second undoubted instance, was thousands of years later in Mezo-America with the Mayan civilization, which had no contact with Mesopotamia. Each of those (between 2-4) isolated inventions of writing systems was not some lightning-strike invention; in each case, it evolved over many hundreds of years and was a collaboration among whole societies, evolving and being modified generation after generation, starting with a few agreed-upon symbols and expanding from there as necessity dictated. None of these original writing systems were "copyrightable." The 20th/21st-century concept of owning certain arrangements of words runs counter to 5,000 years of written language development. Every other alphabet and writing system on the planet is an appropriation of one or more of these original 2-4 systems. The borrowing has been with us from the beginning; "theft" starts at the extreme head waters of the big muddy river:

John Dominic Crossan, *The Historical Jesus* (1991), which is painstakingly researched and shows in great detail how the New Testament is a mash-up of (literally) epic proportions. The Gospels are pretty much collages of many ancient texts, with the older ones being borrowed from and rewritten in the newer ones. The New Testament that people read today is a composite of numerous sources, and in many cases, such as the Gospel of Mark, one ancient writer wrote over the top of a previous one, tacking the whole rising-from the-dead ending onto a previous document that ended without any such miracle.

Shakespeare "plundered" Arthur Brooke's *The Tragical History of Romeus and Juliet* (1562) for his play of (nearly) the same name. Of the 6,000 lines in *Henry VI*, Parts I-III (1591), 4,000 are directly derived from Holinshed's *Chronicles* (1577).

Tchaikovsky's *1812 Overture* (1880) hijacks the French national anthem (1792).

Igor Stravinsky, *The Rite of Spring* (1913). Béla Bartók: "Stravinsky never mentions the sources of his themes. Neither in his titles nor in footnotes does he ever allude to whether a theme of his is his own invention or whether it is taken over from folk music. Stravinsky apparently takes this course deliberately. He wants to demonstrate that it does not matter a jot whether a composer invents his own themes or uses themes from elsewhere. He has a right to use musical material taken from all sources. What he had judged suitable for his purpose had become through this very use his mental property."

Ezra Pound's "creative translation" *Homage to Sextus Propertius* (1919) has done more than any other book to keep alive the poetry of Propertius. Some have criticized Pound's "errors," while others understand that Pound was playing cover versions of the Roman poet and taking liberties as he saw fit.

"Tradition and the Individual Talent" (1919), in which Eliot discusses his theories on influence and borrowing. *The Waste Land* (1922), of course, is composed almost entirely of literary samples, references, and conspicuous assimilations—fragments to shore against his ruins.

Duchamp didn't conceive *Fountain* (1917); nor did he make it. A urinal was art because he said it was. Since Duchamp, what is the nature of art?

Aaron Copeland's *Appalachian Spring* (1944) kidnaps the Shaker melody "Simple Gifts." (1848)

Christian Marclay's *The Clock* is a 24-hour-long video constructed of thousands of film fragments in which a character interacts in some way with a clock or watch. As each new clip appears, a new narrative is suggested, only to be swiftly overtaken by another one. The video is synchronized to the local time. At any moment, I can look at the work and use it as a clock. There are amazingly few kinds of gestures available in the repertory of human behavior, and yet there's a comfort that at, say, 5 p.m. for most people it's quitting time. Film—life itself?—is an irreducibly melodramatic medium. Very, very few clips from comedy would wreck the mood, which is *Our birth is our death begun.* Many of the actors are now dead. Soon enough I'll join them (you, too, dear listener...). The seconds are ticking away as I'm watching. I want to ID the clip—*I exist*—but the fragment and my identification are almost immediately overwhelmed by time, which always wins.

The mimetic function has been replaced by manipulation of the original. Art, not to mention life, now seems to happen primarily in liminal spaces, edited, quoted and quoted again and recontextualized, replaced, collaged, stitched together anew (the stitching together anew is what I really care about).

Examples of collage

Ross McElwee's *Sherman's March* utterly transformed my writing life. By being as self-reflexive as it is, a heat-seeking missile destroying whatever it touches, the film becomes a thoroughgoing exploration of the interconnections between desire, filmmaking, nuclear weaponry, and war, rather than being about only General Sherman.

Amy Fusselman, *The Pharmacist's Mate*. The book fluctuates wildly and unpredictably from Fusselman's attempt to get pregnant through artificial means, her conversations with her dying father, and his WWII diary entries. I don't know what the next paragraph will be, where Fusselman is going, until—in the final few paragraphs—she lands on the gossamer-thin difference between life and death, which is where she's been focused all along, if I could only have seen it.

Maggie Nelson, *Bluets*. A brief meditation on the color blue, a *cri de coeur* about Nelson's inability to get over the end of a love affair, and a grievous contemplation of a close friend's paralysis. The book keeps getting larger and larger until it winds up being about nothing less than the melancholy of the human animal. Why are we so sad? How do we deal with loss? How do we deal with the ultimate loss? It's impressively adult—wrestling with existence at the most fundamental level.

Sarah Manguso's *The Guardians* goes to hell and back, just barely back, and ends with a tiny glimmer of uptick—not too much but not too little, either. It's the only affirmation that anyone can offer: astonishingly, we're here. The book majors in exposed nerve endings. Without which, sorry, I can't read anything. Manguso is mourning both her friend Harris, who on p. 1 commits suicide and herself (she's "dead" now, too). "It doesn't mean shit," an Italian security guard tells her Israeli friend about his passport, which is crucial, since Manguso is always asking, "What if anything means shit?" Nothing does or, rather, everything is shit. How then to put one foot in front of the other? Well, let us investigate that. Life and death are in complete tension (as are Manguso's vow not to make anything up and her acknowledgement that, of course, she will— constantly). I did something I do when I genuinely love a book: start covering my mouth when I read. This is very pure and elemental, and I want nothing coming between me and the page.

Renata Adler's *Speedboat* consists of hundreds of discrete, free-standing, seemingly unrelated paragraphs, all registered in a tone of extraordinarily well-modulated irony. Some of the episodes consist of only a couple of sentences; others are five pages long; most are about half a page. The book is an education in Adler's astringent sensibility, her brutal intelligence. I read her scenes not to find out what will happen but to see if I understand yet what, in Adler's view, constitute the crucial thematic elements of a scene. She repeats the schema over and over until she has taught me how to think about a certain nexus of concerns the same way she does: Language, culture, politics, media, travel, technology are all different kinds of "speedboats"—exciting, unpredictable, powerful, and dangerous in their violent velocity. And just when I've grasped it, the book is over.

As is *Speedboat*, George W.S. Trow's *Within the Context of No Context* is an assemblage of unconnected paragraphs, narrated in a tone of almost fanatical irony, and perhaps best understood as an anthropological autobiography (a term Trow once used to describe his work). In other words, its ostensible accomplishment—a brilliantly original analysis of the underlying grammar of mass culture—is, in a sense, only a way for him to get at his real subject: the world he inhabits (one of absolute irony: no context) and the world his father, a newspaperman, inhabited (one of absolute sentiment: context).

The first piece in Bernard Cooper's *Maps to Anywhere* was select-ed by Annie Dillard as one of the best essays of 1998, but the book as a whole won the PEN/Hemingway Award for the best first novel of 1990, while in the foreword to the book Richard Howard calls the chapters "neither fictions nor essays neither autobiographical illuminations nor cultural inventions." The narrator—Howard calls him "the Bernard-fig-ure (like the Marcel-figure, neither character nor symbol)"—is simultane-ously the "author" and a fictional creation.

From mini-section to mini-section and chapter to chapter, Bernard's conscious and self-conscious attempts to evoke and discuss his own ho-mosexuality, his brother's death, his father's failing health, his parents' divorce, and southern California kitsch are delicately woven together to form an extremely powerful meditation on the relationship between grief and imagination. *"Maps to anywhere"* comes to mean: When a self can (though language, memory, research, and invention) project itself anywhere, and can empathize with anyone or anything, what exactly is a self? The book's final sentences—perfect final sentences particularly important to achieving closure in collage—is an articulation of the mel-ancholy that the narrator has, to a degree, deflected until then: "And I walked and walked to hush the world, leaving silence like spoor."

As are *Speedboat* and *Within the Context of No Context*, Eduardo Ga-leano's *The Book of Embraces* consists of hundreds of extremely short sections; as is *Maps to Anywhere*, it is an ode to the creative imagination's embrace of everything. A mix of memoir, anecdotes, polemic, parablae, fantasy, and Galeano's surreal drawings, the book might at first glance be dismissed as an authorial dumping-ground, but upon more careful inspection, *The Book of Embraces* reveals itself to be virtually a geometric proof on the intertwined themes of love, terror, and imagination.

Brian Fawcett's *Cambodia: A Book For People Who Find Television Too Slow* also blurs fiction and essay. On the top of each page appear para-bles—some fantastic, others quasi-journalistic—all of which are con-cerned with media's colonization of North American life (both Fawcett and Coupland are Canadian). On the bottom of each page, meanwhile, runs a book-length footnote about the Cambodian war. The effect of the bifurcated page is to confront the reader with Fawcett's central motif: wall-to-wall media represents as thorough a raid on individual memory as the Khmer Rouge.

No wonder I'm such a fan of the form and of these books in particular: they're all madly in love with their own crises.

How collage will save your life

We live in a culture that is completely mediated and artificial, rendering us (me, anyway; you, too?) exceedingly distracted, bored, and numb. Straightforward fiction functions only as more bubble wrap, nostalgia, retreat. Why is the traditional novel c. 2013 no longer germane (and the postmodern novel shroud upon shroud)? Most novels' glacial pace isn't remotely congruent with the speed of our lives and our consciousness of these lives. Most novels' explorations of human behavior still owe far more to Freudian psychology than they do to cognitive science and DNA. Most novels treat setting as if where people now live matters as much to us as it did to Balzac. Most novels frame their key moments as a series of filmable moments straight out of Hitchcock. And above all, the tidy coherence of most novels—highly praised ones, in particular— implies a belief in an orchestrating deity or at least a purposeful meaning to existence that the author is unlikely to possess, and belies the chaos and entropy that surround and inhabit and overwhelm us. I want work that, possessing as thin a membrane as possible between life and art, foregrounds the question of how the writer solves being alive. *A book should either allow us to escape existence or teach us how to endure it.* Acutely aware of our mortal condition, I find books that simply allow us to escape existence a staggering waste of time (literature matters so much to me I can hardly stand it).

A student in my class, feeling self-conscious about being much older than the other students, told me he'd been in prison. I asked him what crime he'd committed, and he said, "Shot a dude." He wrote a series of very good but very stoic stories about prison life, and when I asked him why the stories were so tight-lipped, he explained to me the jailhouse concept of "doing your own time," which means that when you're a prisoner you're not supposed to burden the other prisoners by complaining about your incarceration or regretting what you'd done or, especially, claiming you hadn't done it. *Do your own time*: it's a seductive slogan. I find that I quote it to myself occasionally, but really, I don't subscribe to the sentiment. I'm not, after all, in prison. Stoicism is of no use to me whatsoever. What I'm a big believer in is talking about everything until you're blue in the face.

Twenty years ago, Caleb Powell was my undergraduate writing student; we've stayed in touch. I've read and critiqued his essays and stories. A stay-at-home dad and freelance journalist, he's interviewed me occasionally when a new book came out. We disagree about nearly everything. Caleb wanted to become an artist, but he overcommitted to life; I wanted to become a person, but I overcommitted to art. He's one of the most contrary people I've ever met. I like how he questions nearly everything I say. Last fall, we spent a week together in a mountain cabin, recording all of our conversations. We played chess, shot hoops, hiked to lakes and an abandoned mine, dined at a small-town café, relaxed in a hot tub, watched films that featured only two actors locked in struggle, and argued about a multitude of topics: Michael Moore, moral placebos, my high-pitched voice, Jewish identity, transsexual blow jobs, artistic jealousy/envy, DFW, the semicolon, Camus, DJ Spooky, our respective families, Cambodia, racism, capital punishment, et al., inevitably circling back to our central theme of life and art. We went at it hammer and tongs.

In our self-consciousness, we couldn't help but act naturally. Two egos tried to undermine each other. Our personalities overlapped and collapsed. There was no teacher, no student, no interviewer, no interviewee, only a chasm of uncertainty.

We're now trying to turn that uncertainty into art, taking our initial 500,000-word transcript and constructing an argument out of it, a through-line. I love the collage nature of this project, which is a perfect expression of my aesthetic, and I'd even go so far as to say it's an apt metaphor for any writer's artistic process. When you're dealing with such a massive amount of material, you perforce ask yourself, *Isn't this what all writing is, more or less—taking the raw data of the world and editing it, framing it, thematizing it, running your voice and vision over it?* What you're doing is just as much an act of writing, in a way, as it is an act of editing. Multiply 500,000 by a very large number—a trillion, say—and you have the whole of a person's experience (thoughts, anecdotes, misremembered song lyrics, etc.), which he or she then "edits" into art.

I no longer believe in *Great Man Speaks.* I no longer believe in *Great Man Alone in a Room, Writing a Masterpiece.* I believe in art as pathology lab, landfill, recycling station, death sentence, aborted suicide note, lunge at redemption. Your art is most alive and dangerous when you use it against yourself. That's why I pick at my scabs. When I told my friend Michael the title of my forthcoming book, *How Literature Saved My Life,* he said, "Literature never saved anybody's life." It has saved mine—just barely, I think.

I wanted literary collage to assuage human loneliness. Nothing can assuage human loneliness. Literature doesn't lie about this—which is what makes it essential.

Create the World

Douglas Charles Jackson

to write a true
sentence
you must
believe
you can create
the world

because
that is exactly
what you do.

It takes faith, right? You have to believe—when you pick up a pen, open the file, start a story—that you're going to create the world. The first hesitant strokes. A surprising syntax. A fledgling rhythm. And then. And then. And then. A form emerges: land stands in an ocean of silence. Currents push against a theme. A wave swells. The atmosphere thickens and moons orbit in a tidal tug. We're spinning now, and all you can do is grasp for an axis, claw at the core. Write.

CRAFT OF WRITING

The Story of My Writing Career in 3-Act Plot Structure

by Eva Langston

Sometimes it pisses me off that I got my MFA in Fiction Writing so I could learn how to write award-winning, best-selling novels, but all it taught me was how to write short stories for literary magazines.

In my MFA classes we rarely mentioned one of the most important aspects of a novel (or any story, really): the plot. After nearly three years of studying fiction, I sat down to write a novel and realized I still had no idea how to build a book-length story.

Plot seems to be a struggle for a lot of writers. At a large writing conference I attended in Boston a few years ago, all the panels on plot were packed, but even the panelists seemed baffled by the topic. "With my first novel, the structure sort of emerged by accident," one writer said. "Now I'm two hundred and fifty pages into my second novel, and I don't know what the story is. I don't know what I'm doing."

I sat in the audience with my pen poised, ready to take notes, but all of the panelists gave similar, vague anecdotes.

"I write until I see a shape emerge. Then I chip away at it, like a sculptor," one of them said. Some attendees wrote this down in their notebooks. I did not.

Since then I've read a lot of books on story structure. Unlike the conference panelists, the authors of these books are specific and prescriptive. Each has their own tried-and-true plot "formula": the three-act structure, the beat sheet, the cause-and-effect chain. These formulas can be helpful, but sometimes I find myself trying to follow every single guideline from every single book, which is both impossible and paralyzing.

My friend Daniel Wallace (who has a *PhD* in Creative Writing!) once summed up the plot of a good story in a few simple sentences, which he attributed to John Truby's book *The Anatomy of Story*:

A character is morally flawed in some way. At the start of the story, she desperately desires something and struggles to get it, facing increased set-backs. But as she struggles, the evidence accumulates that what she really needs is something more important than getting the thing she desires. Her moral need is what is really at stake, not the thing she desires.

This way of thinking about plot makes sense to me, and it fits with most of the other books on plot I've read over the years. And in thinking about my own flaws and desires, I've decided to put my personal story into a tried-and-true plot formula. Without further ado, here it is:

THE STORY OF EVA'S WRITING CAREER IN THREE ACTS:

ACT 1:

Exposition: Eva has always loved to write and imagines herself a famous, award-winning novelist. At the age of twenty-four, she is confident she will have a book published by the time she turns thirty. After completing her MFA in Fiction, she sits down to write a novel and realizes she has no idea what she's doing. Scared for her future and embarrassed by her lack of success, she becomes a full-time high school math teacher, abandoning writing completely.

Inciting Incident: After two years of teaching (and not writing), Eva turns thirty and feels depressed because she still doesn't have a published novel to her name. She complains on the phone to her high school best friend, Nikki, who then says, "why don't you take some time off and move up here to Cape Cod with me? You can live in my guest room rent-free for a year and be my "writer in residence!""

Debate/Choice/Break into Act 2: Eva thinks about Nikki's offer. Can she really quit her job, put all her possessions in her mother's basement, and go sponge off of her friend for a year? Yes, she decides. She can. She will give herself a chance to make it as a writer, and if she hasn't had success after a year, she'll go back to teaching high school math.

ACT 2:

Setback 1: Eva settles into life with Nikki on the Cape. She rides her bike to the beach, dates a cute lifeguard, and gets a part-time job as a bar trivia hostess. But when she sits down to write, she feels lost and unsure.

Setback 2: In order to mask her difficulties writing, Eva begins accumulating part-time jobs. In addition to bar trivia, she tutors Ukrainians online, creates math curriculum, and works part-time at the liquor store. Now she barely has any time for writing.

Turning Point 1/Momentary Triumph: In a burst of inspiration (and desperation), Eva writes an entire manuscript in a little over a month. On the day she types "THE END" she goes for a triumphant bike ride, imagining that the book will be a huge success and eventually turned into a movie starring Johnny Depp.

Setback 3: Eva starts querying agents with her novel. She gets a few manuscript requests, but ultimately no agents are interested.

Setback 4: Eva revises her novel and queries more agents, but still she gets nothing but rejections. Her year is almost up, and she's no closer to a published novel.

Setback 5: Eva decides not to go back to teaching but instead pieces together part-time jobs and continues to make writing a priority. She moves to Seattle and writes two more novels, both of which are lacking in plot. She feels like a failure. She wonders if she will ever have any success as a novelist or if she should give up and find a different career.

Turning Point 2: Just when all hope seems lost, Eva lands an agent who thinks he can sell the novel she wrote in Cape Cod. Finally, her luck is changing! She and her agent spend the next nine months making revisions, and he encourages her to write a companion book, which she does. Her agent makes a list of New York editors to which he will submit her manuscript. Finally, Eva thinks, I don't have to be embarrassed about my lack of success.

Setback 6: Eva moves to Minneapolis and marries an eccentric scientist. At the wedding, she tells everyone she has an agent and will soon have a book published. But secretly she's worried because her agent has been strangely MIA lately. After returning from her honeymoon, she finally hears from him: he's decided to quit agenting and focus on his own writing. He tells her she's free to take her manuscript and find different representation.

Darkest Moment: Mourning the loss of her agent, Eva begins the querying process all over again. But after more rejections, she looks at her manuscript and sees its many flaws. Most glaringly: the plot is weak. No wonder she's getting nothing but nos. Her friends and family are asking when her book is going to be published, and she has no choice but to say she doesn't know – maybe never. She feels like giving up.

Climax of Act 2: Eva and her husband move to Maryland, and she gets pregnant. How, she wonders, will she be able to juggle a job, a baby, and her writing? Maybe it really is time to put her writing dreams behind her.

Turning Point 3/ Break into Act 3: Eva decides not to give up on writing. If she wants to get another agent, she needs to write a better book. Something that is so good, agents won't be able to reject it. She buckles down and writes another novel, finishing the first draft just weeks before her baby is born.

This is where I am right now in my story. What will happen in Act 3? My friend Daniel says there are several things that can happen at the end of a good story:

1. The protagonist gets the thing she wants but fails to see the moral need. Callous, he says, but perhaps satisfying.
2. The protagonist sees the moral need, changes as a person, and uses her new-found better nature to get the thing she wants. This is a crowd-pleasing success story.
3. The protagonist gives up the search for the thing she wanted and ends up happier for it. This, he says, is a meditative redemption story.

4. The protagonist sees the moral need, gives up the thing she wants, and suffers for losing it. This is a tragedy. (Doing the right thing and suffering for it.)

Of course, I'm hoping that the end of my story will be Option #2. Here is how I imagine it...

ACT 3:

Self-Realization: With a new baby, Eva's priorities and perspectives shift, and she realizes her weakness and flaw: that she has been placing too high of an importance on getting published and having external success. Writing should not be about money or validation or feeling successful. It should be about enjoying the process of creation. She might not publish a novel for quite some time, and that she needs to make peace with that. She needs to stop being ruled by her ego and find joy in her writing, no matter the outcome.

Climax: Once she stops worrying so much about success and what others think of her, Eva begins to enjoy her writing more. It takes many years and a few more failed attempts, but finally she writes a book of which she is proud. Even if agents reject it, she feels *internal* validation for her efforts. And due to her hard work and open heart, the universe smiles on her. She finds a new agent – one who is a better fit than the last one – and her book is published.

New Equilibrium: Eva happily writes more novels, and although she doesn't make much money or win any big awards, she likes her books, and she has a small fanbase who likes them, too. She sometimes gets emails or Twitter shout-outs from readers who tell her how much they enjoy or appreciate her books. The validation is nice of course, but she feels confident about her writing because she has found peace and acceptance from within.

THE END

I suppose this third act I've imagined is wishful thinking, but it's not an impossible dream. It's so hard to stop desiring validation and external success for my writing, but at least I know that's my flaw, so I can try to tame it. I also don't need to *completely* abandon my desire for a published novel. After all, the protagonist's desire is what propels a story forward, and my story still needs a final push towards the finish line.

As far as all the disappointments and setbacks I've encountered, it wouldn't be a good story without obstacles, right? Often, the more setbacks a character faces, the more satisfying the final conclusion.

So I will continue to write novels, and I'm sure I will continue to struggle with plotting, but at least I know this much: give your protagonist something she wants, and don't make it easy for her to get it.

What I Tell Them

Jaswinder Bolina

I'd like to tell them there are too many poets. I'd like to tell them we don't need any more and don't need any more competition. Too many throbbing bodies, not enough room in the bed. I'd like to tell them, you should go to other departments. You should go to the other departments and become exquisite bankers future in-laws will favor. You matter too little, and anyway there isn't any place for poetry. You know too little, what are you doing here?

I don't say these things, though I think sometimes I should. I don't say them because I've seen photographs of Lascaux, so instead, I say, let me tell you about Lascaux and how you and art are irrepressible. I feel wise when I say this, though I'm only twelve or so years removed from where they are now, and I know too little. I tell them this too. I say, I'm only twelve or so years removed from where you are, and I know too little.

Then, there are other things, invented and borrowed, I go ahead and tell them, things I'd like to say in French or in Latin or very cryptically in English as though I'm under incredible strain: You don't matter; only the poem matters. Or, Poems aren't made of ideas, they're made of words, Or, You don't have to be honest, but you have to be sincere.

I don't say any of it in French or in Latin because I never learned enough French or Latin. I don't render it cryptic. I say these things directly because I believe they're true. It's true, I worry I sound didactic or woefully earnest and have embarrassed myself, but then irony would be easier than earnestness, and anyway this isn't about me. Only the poems matter.

I tell them, you are rare people for whom poems matter but, even so, only so rare. After all, I tell them, everybody writes poetry. All of us, in our sentimental, self-important scrawl in hardback, blank journals bought from a rack next to the register in the bookstore. I have those journals too. They're in a box under the folding table I use for a desk.

I take them out and, embarrassed, tear out a few pages every so often. Entire books eventually disappear. Everyone writes poetry, I tell them, which is why there's a place for it, and you have these journals too, but you're rare people for going public with this information.

I tell them, by going public with this information, you agree to the term and condition that your poetry is no longer your own. Sure, we talk to ourselves, and we write notes to ourselves, but no-one writes poetry to himself, herself, oneself. You might write *for* yourself, but you write *to* somebody else. You should be nice to that person. That person is seated beside you. Say hello.

But this person isn't enough. You want somebody else. I tell them, you want the somebody who would stroll into a library in Tucson or Greenwich on a Wednesday and find what you've written. You want that person to pull you down off a shelf in the future and open you up and marvel. You want to be somebody's afternoon reading on the veranda, somebody's Xerox hung with a tack on the inspiring wall.

I tell them that much is possible, but what you write here won't appear in the *Norton*. No editor will call you. For that sort of thing to happen, you have to walk into a library, open a book of poems, and marvel. You have to do this several times a month—several times a week if you have time—over many years. You'll need to paper your wall.

What you write between treks to the library will disappear under the folding table, and you'll reach for it every so often and, embarrassed, discard a few pages until entire books disappear. Some of it, though, you'll keep, and some of it might find a way to a shelf and to somebody else. That much is possible, I tell them. Some of it will congeal and assemble.

I tell them the trick is entirely in language. Poems are made out of words, and these words need to be your own. Your words are what sincerity is made from, I tell them, and in this you have all you need for poetry. I tell them, use the words you remember from cartoons, words from your mother speaking of rutabaga, from your chemistry tutor and the redhead who at first ignored you, the words you think of when you think of the bodega on Granville and yourself later naked in the redhead's apartment. These words are yours, and your poems should be made out of them.

I give them examples. I tell them, our 'morning' is always 'frigid' and 'gray,' our 'clothing' was always 'ragged' and 'torn,' and our 'fingers' are always 'stained' 'with' 'tobacco,' the 'fingers' 'of' 'smoke' 'caressing' 'the' 'light bulb.'

I tell them, your morning should be 'neurons' and 'steam.' You should arrive in a 'smock' or in 'machinist's regalia.' You needn't bother with smoking and fingers, we've had enough of cigarettes in poetry. Your words need to supplant our words so we can arrive at knowledge and also discover we know too little. It will be startling.

Your task is to arrange these words strangely in order to explain more clearly what happened. Your task is to help us understand what happened, I tell them, but what happened isn't always simply the facts. What happened isn't always a story. Sometimes, it's just some images. Sometimes, it's entirely sound.

To figure out which it is, I tell them, you'll need to let the poem overthrow you. It's made of words, and even if they're your words, they're part of language, and language is much bigger than you. Naturally, this will generate some conflict. The poem will sometimes need to be silent where you want to speak, or it'll need to be explicit where you turn to muttering. It will be confused about what you know for certain or certain about what confuses you. Sometimes, the poem will sputter and quit no matter how hard you admire or kick it. Sometimes, it neglects you completely, and this, I tell them, is okay.

You're here to relinquish, I tell them. You're here to sever a nerve.

Holding a Paper Clip in the Dark
Matthew Zapruder

When someone asks me how I start writing, I'm never sure exactly how to answer. I guess the best way to describe it would be as a mostly formless impulse to start working with language, until I feel that electric charge that happens when I put words together in a way that starts to make a poem. If I have an idea or a desire, it's almost always nothing more than a notion to see what happens if I start playing around with a certain word, what sorts of things will start to come up. It's probably more than anything just about as stupid and idea-less as groping in the dark with a paper clip, looking to stick it into an electrical outlet.

Often what seems to work is to start with a question, a specific one, in the rhetorical sense, one that I can actually ask myself, out loud. As those of us who teach know, asking a simple question in class to a group of students about a text or life can create an interesting place to explore, a field of possibility. The more literal this field is the better (sometimes it's even an actual field!). Sometimes it's worth moving into, most of the time it turns out it wasn't, but if I sit and work long enough something will start to happen. And then, miraculously, that will unexpectedly lead to the biggest issues in one's life.

Again, maybe that makes it sound like I start with an idea. I don't. Usually it's an impulse, or maybe just a situation or collection of words that seems promising. Over the years of writing, I've gotten a little better at being able to see those moments of possibility that actually have something in them, and to reject those moments that might seem cool or interesting but are actually just shallow and boring.

How I move through the poem usually is mostly a matter of following what is interesting and meaningful. More groping. Sometimes it's only that, but at other times there's some structure in the groping, even if it's kind of arbitrary, that can help lead to something. Here's an example of a poem I wrote that way:

THE ELEGANT TROGON

The South American trogon
is a gentle bird with weak legs
and soft colorful feathers
that nibbles holes in trees
to make its nest. One flew
into my dream and dropped
a golden tooth into my supinate
hand, then perched croaking
on a twig. It appeared
to be wearing spectacles.
Special effects, said a Spadefoot,
digging calmly as a scholar
of the Era of Good Feelings.
I felt a rictus travel across
my face, arriving at my mouth
in the form of an effortful
grimace. Dawn was carrying
something quantum in its oral
cavity and purring. I have
a secret pigeon in my heart.
I keep it in a cage composed
of object lessons and feed it
moral law. Usually every morning
it stirs and wakes me with
its lonely cooing and together
we wander into a sort of
guilty state of already feeling
as if we are at loggerheads
with the turtle of doing what
we ought to do. Now I am
fully awake. Still I feel that golden
lodestone burning in my palm.

Which I plan on keeping locked.

The Elegant Trogon is, obviously, a type of bird. I wrote this poem
as I often do, using a process: I began with a task that is purely mechanical, designed to produce words or phrases that must be used in
the poem. In "The Elegant Trogon," I began in a certain place in the
dictionary, and chose words moving backwards through the book until

I reached another specified point. This process was shamelessly stolen directly from the one my friend Matthea Harvey invented to create the stunning sections *Terror of the Future* and *The Future of Terror* in her amazing book, *Modern Life*.

I required myself, as Matthea did, to use the words in the order I found them. To be honest I can't remember what the exact original starting and ending words were, but along the way I came across the words trogon, tooth, supinate, spectacles, special effects, spadefoot, rictus, quantum, oral cavity, object lessons, moral law, loggerheads, lodestone, locked.

After I do the process and generate the "raw material," I come up with a subject or situation along which I can string those words in a way that feels natural and authentic.

I really like the simultaneous centripetal and centrifugal feelings of these words that want to go in different directions, but also somehow always seem to, in the end, belong together. I have certain nearly religious beliefs about language: that it expresses the collective historical intelligence of human beings, and that it is the accumulated wisdom of all language users. Therefore, I also have a great faith that my little humanity, plus the great wisdom of language, in the right combination and with the right degree of humility and attention on my part, will result in poems.

I had no idea what I was going to write the poem "about." Such an attitude toward my process would I think have been inimical to true discovery of my subject, what was mattering to me in a way I could not see until I wrote the poem. I just tried to pick words that seemed interesting and had a lot of different possibility, but also specificity. Once I looked up the first word, trogon, and saw that there was a type called Elegant, I began to build something, and both use, and be moved around by, each subsequent word I chose.

This is a not uncommon way for me to write poems, but it's not the only way I write them. It's best when I just sit down in the morning—either at a desk if I'm not traveling, or at a café, hopefully in a sunny spot where there is some but not too much conversation and music, and see what starts to happen.

A lot of the time I try to take a phrase or object that is particularly relevant to my daily surroundings, and use it as an anchor for further meditation. I find the tension between daily life and all the thoughts we have moving through it to be particularly significant for me as a human being.

What do I want? I want you (the reader) to look at these poems as places that feel to me private to my own experience yet also common to all of our experiences. That is, they are very particular moments but ones that hopefully feel somewhat familiar. Maybe each of the poems—all of its words, building an experience for the reader to visit and move through—is just a very long name for an emotion we all have felt but have not heard named until that moment.

And then there is the matter of how to end. I don't personally believe the end of the poem needs to be characterized by a state of relatively greater understanding of the initial question or set of concerns. Rather, I think that along the way there are various states of understanding, openings-up of new concerns that emerge from what was being talked about before. Sort of like how a conversation with a friend might move as opposed to a lecture. So along the way we know more about some questions, and have some new ones.

I ended the poem "Aglow" with the following lines:
> it has been a hidden pleasure but mostly an awful pain talking to you
> with a voice that pretends to be shy and actually is, always in search of the
> question that might make you ask me one in return.

To put it simply, I sit down and write and if it seems like a voice emerges that is caring about something, I struggle for some period of time (sometimes a few minutes, sometimes days or weeks or months or years) to find the right way of putting words down that allows that speaker to be authentically alive in the poem. When I feel comfortable, I know I have found the right solution. But I try not to have any preconceptions about how the poem ought to look in relation to other poems I have written or what I imagine I am or should be doing. The voice in the poem absolutely must feel full and alive and human to me.

I think a lot about the following very famous passage from William Carlos Williams's introduction to his 1944 book, *The Wedge*: "As in all machines its [poetry's] movement is intrinsic, undulant, a physical more than a literary character. In a poem this movement is distinguished in each case by the character of the speech from which is arises."

In other words, the poem is a kind of organic machine that arises to "do" what is necessary given whatever the voice that is speaking needs it to do.

I think I know the poem is done when I get another electric charge, something like Emily Dickinson's "physical feeling as if the top of my head were taken off." The poem's not something that belongs to me, or that I even feel like I've "done." I feel like the poem is something that language, our common possession, has made through its particular instrument, me.

Dispelling the Myth of the Poet: Why Poets Need to Defend the Craft
Lisa Marie Basile

I tried to dispel the Myth last night at a house party. I think it went well.

Picture this: Me, an investment banker, a real estate agent, an ads man, and an environmental scientist. The ads man was happy, quite happy, to take home $100k per year. Hard work, but not soul-sucking. The investment banker said that you have to work soullessly until you're 45 to see the real financial benefits, but by that time you're alone, miserable, and work-obsessed. The environmental scientist said she wanted so badly to make a difference, but politics gets in the way. She was happy, though. She was a happy human. When they asked me what I did, they were confused. "You mean, like, poetry poetry?"

Could I also be happy doing this archaic, gilded thing? Am I a reincarnated soul from the belle époque? What does it even mean to be a poet today? Do I write song lyrics? What do I do for a job? Surely there are no minstrels. Do I sit in cafes? After a long day do I come home and write down my feelings?

Feelings.

I do not blame people for their lack of understanding. I do not blame people for their stereotypes, especially when the cinematic image of The Poet has been crammed into one tiny, silly little baroque box of poverty and tears and romance and melodramatics and black cloaks. How could I blame the media? They want their easy depictions and can't be bothered with anything else. Even I was reduced to being a contemporary "young woman poet" writing about "menstruation, orgasms, and lady parts" in a feature printed in, of all places, the New York Daily News. Now, I don't believe I have even one poem about menstruation, but so it goes. Rudimentary, innocuous, superficial. Do poets not deserve better?

So, it's me, the banker, the ads guy, and the scientist. They're all over-educated and working hard. When you are an educated individual who spends countless dollars on schooling, you expect that most other people are or were following a similar trajectory: University > Job > Life. Accomplishment is found in the dollar, but it is not found in creation.

The Poet's life is a different animal. It is not so black and white, but that doesn't mean it's not calculated or purposeful. Often redefined as a nighttime passion that takes backseat to one's "real job," the Poet is by default reduced to hobbyist. The conventional path may have been taken, just as it may have been forsaken. For me, the Poetry has not followed school and is a real job. I didn't graduate into a life of poetry and I am not my job. In fact, I feel my poet-self watching from above me at my cubicle at work, saying, "Get out of there." I am just going through the motions in order to live.

I am Lisa and I contribute in a variety of other ways (if we must derive value from the idea of contributions). Sure, there's a day job, but I also write, edit, and publish work as a poet. I do not moonlight as a poet. Poetry is a sort of job like many others. Unlike the investment banker, though, I do not subscribe to the belief that any pedagogy—learning and writing within the structures of the MFA, alongside a famous mentor, or while studying the canon—makes a Poet. It does not require a background. I believe that a Poet is made by lifestyle and dedication.

My diagnosis is that people put "art" and "life" into two separate boxes. Therefore, the problem is that the Poet in Society is seldom heard or taken seriously at large, because our "box" is the "other" box, the seemingly intangible place that you can opt out of.

"I haven't read poetry since college," the banker told me. I say, "I have never known anything about banking besides how to check my bank account." Yet his job is respected and coveted and mine is the catalyst for an amused conversation. Like a parent shooing a child: "Aw, that's so cute!" I am suddenly the odd one out. I perhaps am strange. So be it, I'm strange. But that's not all of me. It's not all of you, either.

So, you all know it: When you say that you are a poet, the retorts are plentiful. Many are ignorant but of course forgivable. Many others are reductive to the point of being insulting. For whatever reason, the Poet's work seems to have been both diminished to that of a drippy college elective (made worse by the canonical white hetero-normative selections) and a personal hobby caused by depression and melodrama. And Feelings. As though poetry doesn't require craft, knowledge and observation of sound, culture, identity, social spheres, space, and language. As though it isn't its own variety of reportage, a record of what isn't being said.

According to Ann Rene Johnson, over at Johns Hopkins School of Education:

> Former President John F. Kennedy stated, "I see little of more importance to the future of our country and of civilization than full recognition of the place of the artist. If art is to nourish the roots of our culture, society must set the artist free to follow his/her vision wherever it takes him/her." Beverly Sills is noted for her powerful quote "Art is the signature of civilization."
>
> Webster's Dictionary helps to give greater meaning to these profound statements. Community is defined as—"Society at large." Value is defined as—"Something intrinsically valuable or desirable." Belief is defined as: "Something believed." Education comes from the Latin root "educare" to lead out or draw from. What we know to be true, throughout history, is that the ARTS—all of them, are beliefs and values in all societies that lead out, or draw from each of us—the art from within. The ARTS define and celebrate all aspects of our lives. The ARTS are the universal language that communicates to all peoples. That is why the arts continue—they are values and beliefs. Values and beliefs are the very essence of who we are, and how we behave. Values and beliefs are constant in a changing world and society. The arts capture our essence, our purpose, our world, through multi medium experiences that communicate and transcend to all cultures in all languages.

Johnson hit the nail on the head. Art—including the entirety of poetry (no matter the clique to which a poem may belong)—Is Not Private. Poets don't write poetry in notebooks late at night only to never show a soul. That is a person who writes poetry. There is a difference, and this is why our jobs must be respected.

The Poet and Their Poetry are a public entity that have observed, eaten, digested, analyzed, broken, re-appropriated, questioned, re-questioned, loved, hated, assaulted, calculated, and regurgitated society and community as a whole, even if that society and that community is one human being affected within it.

The ads man, the investment banker, the scientist, and the real estate agent all asked me, "So, what do you do as a poet?" I told them I read, write, edit, publish, study, promote, and share my work and the work of others. They asked me if I got paid. If I wrote when I was sad. That they thought it must be hard to be a "struggling poet." That most poets are "little wimps." I told them: I'm not struggling. I'm not a wimp. I get paid. And that I often write when I am happy and balanced.

I think it is of utmost importance that we defend and share our poetry with the outside world. We must believe in and populate the world with the worth of our work. I will say that the intrinsic nature of the poetry "scene" (and its various arms) is a glorious thing at times. We as poets (even with the nepotism, ego, clique, and jealousy) care deeply for one another; we appreciate and see the time and obsession we all share, whether we like the "other" work or not. But poetry ought not be self-contained. A little mystery is a good thing, but sharing is better. Don't you think your work deserves it?

We must take a step outside of this realm. When you're at a party, a family gathering, a wedding, a bar—wherever people might ask you about life as a poet—be honest: tell them about your work. Don't self-deprecate. Defend the countless hours, the late-nights wading through Submittable submissions, the pain and glory of rejections and acceptances.

Tell them about why you write, why it matters and why it has an impact. Don't settle for hobbyist because it's easy to explain. Tell them that poets aren't all wimpy and sad. Tell them about the anthologies you edit, the courses you teach, the readings you do, the readings you host, the conferences you attend, the fellowships that allow you to see the world, the contest you won, and the book being published. Don't talk down to them. When they ask you, "what's your poetry about?" don't water it down. Let it speak for itself. This is something most poets find difficult, because how do you explain white space and theory? You just do. Just try. Trust your audience in the making.

When you're an ads man, a banker, and a scientist, you are legitimized. You're contributing to society in a verifiable way. These jobs are transactions-based. They can be measured in revenue and developments. But poetry, too, is a tangible job and craft. It is simultaneously immortal and ever-changing. It will live longer than a bank account. It really is the art that begs of the Poet to have the same skill-sets that are so rewarded in society: the knowledge of analysis, research, devotion, marketing, and creativity. But there's some other intangible element, too, and that's what sets us apart. Don't deny that.

Say it.

Beyond the Plot Triangle
Maya Sonenberg

Fiction writers learn that plot's the norm and all other forms abnormal, but I've always been entranced by other forms, never really loved plot. And yet I've worried—why plot, why not, and what else instead?

According to E. M. Forster, plot is "a narrative of events, the emphasis falling on causality."[1] He was irked by narrative and yet he found it necessary: "It runs like a backbone—or may I say a tapeworm, for its beginning and end are arbitrary," he wrote.[2] Why did he—and why have we—come to view the inverted triangle of exposition, conflict, complications, climax, and resolution as the necessary skeleton for all fiction? In their introduction to *Extreme Fiction*, Michael Martone and Robin Hemley note that "the realist writer seeks to create an illusion so perfect that the reader cannot tell it is an illusion. The reader observes the action as it takes place in real space and in real time. The story unfolds before our eyes…The realist story wants you, the reader, to forget you are reading."[3]

Perhaps as we've come to associate plot with realism, we've come to believe that plot is as necessary and natural as our own bodies: the bones of events connected by the ligaments of cause and effect; the vivid descriptions, natural-sounding dialogue, and detailed actions fleshing out the basic form, as muscles pad our bones; the themes and meanings nestling deep inside, the way our most important organs— heart, liver, and lungs—are protected by our muscles and bones; and the clear but lively sentences encasing all the rest, the way our skin encases us. Or maybe plot is the bicycle below the body instead. A steady plod of gears creaking through cause and effect, climbing that mountain towards the one and only inevitable climax, after which it's all downhill. But what if I turn away from plot, natural or not? Why might I be spellbound by not-plot instead?

One: I'm bad at plot. I admit it. Although I can appreciate the intricacies of a good plot and understand how deeply a plot can be a metaphor (all the actions, interactions, causes and—particularly—effects working to dramatize a story's beating heart), and although I've gotten better at writing plot over the years, I'm still bad at it, dumb in fact. When I was a graduate student, teachers lost patience with my forays into other forms and one finally said to me, "Characters in action, Maya. We need characters in action!" I went right home and wrote a story about people dancing all night in a punk club—this was the 1980s after all, and those characters were certainly active. When I brought that story in, though, he just said, "No. The Bouncer needs to ask her to marry him." Only years later did I understand what he meant: characters *interacting*, the basis for plot in most contemporary literary fiction.

Two: I was raised on abstraction. My parents, both painters, took me to museums and galleries nearly every Saturday. When I wasn't playing with the sand in the ashtrays, I looked at the abstract expressionist paintings of Pollock and Rothko and the minimalist sculpture of Donald Judd and Carl Andre, and so the norm—my norm—was to see art as material-based, self-referential, intellectual, and emotional, rather than realistic or narrative. Painting says something about canvas and paint, frame and rectangle; if a Rothko painting says something about the world beyond itself, it does so in a metaphorical, spiritual, or philosophical way. By extension, literature is about words, not the world—at least not literally. When I started writing fiction, I sensed intuitively that "realism creates a highly crafted aesthetic literary artifact that [only] appears to be spontaneous" and that "transparency is the camouflage of realism."[4]

Three: If fiction *is* some sort of window on or mirror of the world, plot is not the world. While we live and die chronologically, experience cause and effect, and at least some of our actions have consequences—"daily life," as E. M. Forster wrote, "is... full of the time-sense"[5] — life is not a neat string of these interactions, not a set of neatly interlocking gears. Even if Newton's Third law is true for physics (*when one body exerts a force on a second body, the second body exerts a force equal in magnitude and opposite in direction to that of the first body*), it does not necessarily apply

---

[1] E. M. Forster, *Aspects of the Novel* (San Diego, New York, London: Harcourt Brace & Company, 1927), 86.

[2] Ibid., 26.

[3] Robin Henley and Michael Martone, "Introduction" in Extreme Fiction: Fabulists and Formalists (New York, Pearson Longman, 2004), 3.

to human interaction. One human action may have many consequences, and even an action we think should be hugely consequential may have few interesting consequences. For example, it is possible, though horrendous, to imagine a murder with no consequences beyond the obvious one—that the victim is dead.

Well beyond grad school, even after I'd learned to recognize plot and to write one, I was still uninterested in it. Writing about mothering young children and caring for aging parents at the same time, I saw how plot truly can't convey all the facets of human life we might want to write about. With its neatly building complications, its single climax, and its resolution, plot couldn't possibly help me write about the simultaneous boredom, joy, angst, anger, and sleep deprivation that marked my experience of mothering; nor could it help me write about watching my father sink through dementia into a second infancy. I could have created stories with tidy plots and neat trajectories in which a baby grows up nicely due to the mother's ministrations or grows up badly due to her neglect, or in which a daughter comes to realize and accept her father's limitations, and I could even have drawn a nice parallel—children and grandfather reversing roles and leading to the mother-daughter's sure epiphany— but the form itself felt falsely mechanical, at odds with experiences in which the miserable and the joyful, the dutiful and the resentful, existed simultaneously and circularly. The cause of the father's stroke (a blood clot moving to the brain during open heart surgery) was only of medical interest, and the causes of the children's personalities and actions were mysterious and complex, beyond their parents' control. Emotions, events, and personalities swirled, repeated, co-existed, and flip-flopped, rather than culminated in a climax during which one "won out" over the others. Undoubtedly, I'm simplifying plot—the best don't bare their bones so easily—but, still, I needed to jettison plot before I could figure out what these stories meant to me and what they might mean to others.

Even if realism is in fact camouflage and plot is in fact artifice rather than a force of nature, just as limited and arbitrary and wonderful as the sonnet, plot also provides two useful things: armature and engine, structure to give shape to fiction and a force to move the story along.

---

4 Ibid., 3.

5 Forster, 28.

Thoughtfully jettisoning plot requires replacements—strategies for finding alternative forms and a new encyclopedia of forms to draw from, a new kind of body and a new kind of bike.

I'm not alone in spurning plot, of course. Fiction writers have used a myriad of other forms to shape and steer their work: Myla Goldberg's comprehension test, Lily Hoang's I Ching, Julio Cortazar's *Hopscotch*, Milorad Pavic's crossword puzzles and lexicons, Tina May Hall's crown of sonnets and Rick DeMarinis's villanelle, Susan Neville's "Rondo," Eleanor Henderson's Mad Libs, and all the works of the Oulipo, the Ouvroir de Littérature Potentielle (Workshop of Potential Literature). This loose gathering of mainly French-speaking writers, founded in 1960, still uses constrained writing techniques to create fiction: abstract, practically mathematical sets of rules. Some Oulipian constraints include the N+7, in which every noun is replaced with the seventh noun after it in a dictionary, and the Lipogram, in which a piece of writing excludes one or more letters. The most famous example of this is Georges Perec's novel *A Void*, which lacks the letter "e." These forms are both playful and challenging, and poets already know that such fixed forms are anything but frivolous. Constraint leads to generation, and so I followed the poets and began using fixed verse forms to generate fiction I hoped would more deeply engage both the head and the heart.

It all started with the skeleton of a sperm whale suspended below a balcony. Its gigantic empty head seemed the perfect metaphor for my father's mind after his stroke and for the miserable impossibility of making contact with him. Staring down at the skeleton, I felt that upwelling, that pressure, that irresistible urge to shape the scene, to write. I tried memoir, then a traditional plotted story, and then fiction in collage form, only to be confounded each time. The material pushed back against all my attempts to wrangle it into place, and I finally threw up my hands and thought, "Why not? Let's try a sonnet!" It would have been easy enough to set up some arbitrary equivalents (stanza=paragraph, line=sentence, rhyme=rhyme), but the meaningful units of poems and stories are different. The paragraph isn't really the equivalent of a stanza, nor the sentence the equivalent of the line, and a rhyme at the end of every sentence oddly breaks momentum in prose, and so I considered the basics of this form,

the sonnet—its stanzas, its lines, its rhymes—and drew some other paral-
lels: a scene would be the meaningful unit, similar to a stanza, and so the
story would have four scenes; a paragraph would stand in for a line; and
an image for a rhyme but not always at the end of a line. In shaping these
essential elements (certainly ones I'd used before) in a new way, I found
that I could both control and convey the material's wild emotions. And
the sharp "turn," or volta, a sonnet takes near its end changed my main
character's thinking about all the events of the story, bringing me close
to creating a plot after all—volta as epiphany that springs not from the
logic of cause and effect but from the lyric of image, the oscillation of
repetition and variation, the swing of song and sense.

This one poem-story pushed me, and I tumbled down some rabbit
hole. I couldn't resist. I couldn't stop writing in form. I tried a sestina,
but rather than repeating the end-words of lines, I rotated six "standard"
elements of fiction through the traditional pattern like carousel horses:
character, point of view, conflict, setting, image, and action. With each
spin of the platform, I learned something new: it is really difficult to
write conflict before character, character before point of view, action
before image. Then I tried a villanelle, in which the insistent repetitions
embodied the pressures a woman feels listening to her senile mother and
her whining toddler at the same time. Then the looping repetitions of
a pantoum haunted another woman as she cleaned out her dead mother's apartment and prevented her from throwing all those belongings
out the window. The repetitions of a rondeau rudely pushed the female
narrator's past life into her present, until she seemed to have no choice
but to return home and murder a man she'd hoped she'd forgotten, the
father of her current lover. A haiku cycle spun easily through seasons,
but forced me away from my usual reliance on metaphor and taught me
just how deeply metaphor is embedded in the English language. For example, in what ways is the following phrase a metaphor: the baby's breath
freezes and furs immediately on her scarf?

In some of these stories form is residual, the ghost of scaffolding,
but in others, the form is insistent, like flying buttresses, the supports still
visible and fully incorporated into the architecture, even once the build-

ing is complete. In all cases, form brought puzzling human moments into sharper focus and pressured me to ask deeply about writing. How can lyric create movement from first page to last, alongside or without narrative? What can I learn about a verse form by hassling it with extremely emotional content and what can I learn about the content of my stories by applying pressure to it with form? What can I learn about the most essential elements of fiction? What can I learn about my own writing habits and what can I learn by being forced to break those habits? These questions have felt at times game-like, hypothesis-like, philosophical, studious, scientific, metaphysical, theoretical, but the answers, provisional though they might be, have never been frivolous.

On Being Lazy, Or, What I'm Doing This Summer

Lindsay Illich

Reading and thinking and writing set off a buzz, the mind at full tilt doing its thing. Engaging with words is the self as aural archive, making one function of invention curatorial, a gleaning of voices among the sheaves of ambient glossolalia. It's in those echoes a writer hums like a tuning fork, her scalp razed. The problem is, if it's a problem at all, is that most of this stuff happens inside your head. Interiority, no matter how verdant and lush, is hard to explain. And for me, I have to remind myself that what looks like laziness (and sometimes feels like laziness) isn't laziness at all but the loam of creative soil.

Some of the ambivalence about the status of writing as work comes from the literary tradition, a strain in poetics, especially the generative aspects, that insists on what seems superficially as passivity, even laziness. Think Keats's diligent indolence, Whitman's loafing and indirection, Emerson's "blithe spirit" trolling Boston Common. What has been misunderstood about loafing and indirection is the implied engagement with the world as the *a priori* of composing: loafing isn't laziness—it is liberating engagement, the freedom to be enlivened by the world in whatever way you choose.

Another source about the status of writing comes from the American tradition, beginning as early as Benjamin Franklin. Recall, from his *Autobiography*, Franklin's companion James Ralph who traveled with him to London. Repeatedly, Franklin discourages Ralph's literary pursuits, particularly because Ralph received little if any monetary compensation for his work. In the context of the *Autobiography*, Franklin's criticisms amount to a critique of laziness; more specifically, Franklin's critique rests on a root metaphor: *time is money*.

Is it any surprise to learn that laziness as a moral failing was a preoccupation of American literature? Washington Irving's "Rip Van Winkle: A Posthumous Writing of Diedrich Knickerbocker" begins curiously with a paragraphs-long parenthetical note on the origins of the story, explaining how the recently dead gentleman Knickerbocker collected oral histories among the old burghers of the Catskills. The narrator notes uncharitably that Knickerbocker's time "might have been much better employed in weightier labors," speculating that Knickerbocker's shot at immortality is slim to none: he will be remembered for as long as it takes to digest a biscuit, thinks the narrator. The unnamed narrator dismisses Knickerbocker, characterizing his work as a folklorist as useless, thus framing one of the first American short stories as a cautionary tale about a scholar wasting his life caring about something that didn't matter to anyone else (how's that for self-reflexive irony?). Here's a litmus test for your sensitivity to these criticisms: how do you feel when someone describes your work as "esoteric?"

Then, in Knickerbocker's words, we learn of the story's protagonist, Rip Van Winkle:

> The great error in Rip's composition was an insuperable aversion to all kinds of profitable labor. It could not be from the want of assiduity or perseverance; for he would sit on a wet rock, with a rod as long and heavy as a Tartar's lance, and fish all day without a murmur, even though he should not be encouraged by a single nibble. He would carry a fowling piece on his shoulder, for hours together, trudging through woods and swamps, and up hill and down dale, to shoot a few squirrels or wild pigeons. He would never even refuse to assist a neighbor in the roughest toil, and was foremost a man at all country frolics for husking corn, or building stone fences. The women of the village, too, used to employ him to run their errands, and to do such little odd jobs as their less obliging husbands would not do for them; in a word, Rip was ready to attend to anybody's business but his own; but as to doing family duty, and keeping his farm in order, it was impossible.

Rip didn't care about money. He wasn't lazy or weak; he attended patiently to the children of the community, helped local farmers with construction and harvest, and obliged their wives' honey-do lists. He hiked about, preferred the company of his dog or his friends at the tavern, where they discussed politics and philosophy, or, if they were lucky, the news from a newspaper left by a traveler.

We know the rest of the story: out hunting, Rip hears someone calling his name: "Rip Van Winkle! Rip Van Winkle!" The caller is a Dutchman dressed in the old style, needing help hauling some kegs of beer. When the chore is done, they offer Rip a cold one. Being a "thirsty soul," he accepts, then has another, and then, finding himself suddenly sleepy, dozes.

Upon waking, the mountain landscape is the same, but everything else is different. His dog gone and gun rusty, Rip heads into town where he discovers King George's portrait replaced by George Washington's. His children are grown, his daughter married to one of the orphans he nurtured before his long sleep. His wife, the queen of the totalitarian regime Rip knew as matrimony ("petticoat government") was dead, having blown an aneurism during an argument with a shoe repairman.

For those engaged in the kind of soulful and intellectual work that requires study and contemplation—the kind of dwelling in possibility that sometimes means, from an outsider's perspective, that nothing is getting done—"Rip Van Winkle" offers a beautiful allegory. We reap what we sow, eventually. In what feels like one day, Rip sees the outcomes of his cumulative days: from the philosophical talks at the tavern with concerned colonists emerge revolution and democracy; an urchin he cared for becomes a responsible husband and father; and, well, Irving kills off Rip's spousal taskmaster. "Rip Van Winkle" is Frank Capra's *It's a Wonderful Life* in reverse: here, look at the bounty of your labors for having cared for those around you and for being engaged with the world.

As an aside, It's a Wonderful Life was based on the short story "The Greatest Gift," by Philip Van Soren Stern. He wrote the story as the text of a Christmas card he sent out to friends and relatives in 1943. Stern was a Civil War historian and editor of the letters of Lincoln and the work of Poe and Thoreau. I wonder what Ben Franklin might have said to Stern as he wasted his time composing Christmas cards for his loved ones?

It's this story I want to tell the people who ask me what I'm doing this summer, at least the ones who do so to indict my laziness. I would tell them these things, give them my copy of Lewis Hyde's *The Gift*. Washington Irving's labors were not lost any more than Capra's or Sterns or mine have been this afternoon, or, for that matter, yours, for reading this.

We say of a letter, remark, or conversation, *that was touching*. It's a common idiom, but one that speaks truth about the connection between words and the body: affect is embodied the same way writing is, the body a bellwether for the right words. In *Light Years*, James Salter remarks of words: "The power to change one's life comes from a paragraph, a lone remark. The lines that penetrate us are slender, like the flukes that live in river water and enter the bodies of swimmers." Just as metaphors transform vehicle and tenor, words change writers and readers, and this is the real work of the world—conquering estrangement, bridging the gap between points of view. Something happens. In other contexts, we call it falling in love; it's a leap, the transformative plunge into empathy.

But none of this happens without time dedicated to reading and thinking and writing.

If you are a writer who lives with non-writers, and those non-writers are what I would call *doers*—that is, people who tend to be happiest when the body is occupied in some purposeful activity (raking leaves, folding laundry, scooping snow, weeding the strawberry patch, running, baking, pinning more things to do on Pinterest)—there's a good chance you've been called out for what appears to the busy bees of the world as "doing nothing." I am especially conscious of this appearance when I'm with family in Nebraska, third generation farmers whose daily chores require the caloric intake of a moose. It makes me want to wear a T-shirt that says something like, IT MAY NOT LOOK LIKE IT TO YOU, BUT I'M WORKING.

What I'm doing this summer is vacating the idea of busy-ness. Summer is a laptop in bed, arrays of open books, a window unit AC blasting on me. The sheets are red and white paisley hand-me-downs, cast-offs from my sister who used my move to Boston as an excuse to upgrade hers. I'm reading a biography of Marianne Moore (nicknamed by mother and brother "Rat" from the *The Wind in the Willows*), Kierkegaard, tons of Mo

Willems, Ian Bogost, Studs Turkel.

It worries me that the gift economies of art are losing value, that reading for many is a luxury when it has counted as the thing that for me set the world to technicolor, that the "time as money" metaphor is so powerful that we think of a day as "wasted" when we indulge in reading and thinking and writing. There are few answers, except to do more reading and thinking and writing. By these we are humbled and enlarged in equal measure, a beating heart that for me is iambic.

So that's what I'm doing this summer.

Calling Bullshit On A Writer's Top 10 Excuses For Not Writing

Peter Mountford

1. No one will want to read it.

Yeah, that's probably true. It'll get better, probably, eventually. First, you'll show your mama, and she'll tell you it's good. This does not actually mean it's good, quite yet. Then, your friends will tell you the next one is good. They might be wrong or right, depending on how honest they are. Finally, strangers will tell you it's good. And last, people will actually pay to read your writing, because they want to read it. This process can take anywhere between a few months to several decades. Good luck!

2. I don't have time.

I may be wrong, but I suspect your problem is that you have a life. Do away with that. Like, adios to yoga and the gym, plus stop jogging, Pinteresting, sky-diving, stamp-collecting, and so on. Facebook and other social media are cool in moderation, I think, but just keep the writing document open and it'll glare at you angrily the whole time. Or write longhand. It sounds weird to youngsters, but it's actually really good; most of the best stuff I've written started longhand. I guess a lot of the bad stuff I've written was done longhand, too.

Most relationships are overrated, or they don't have to be so time consuming at least, so do the bare minimum (or less), to maintain civil relations with the people whom you value the most. TV's out, of course, unless it's late and you're really comatose after a lot of work, in which case you're not good for much anyway.

Guess what? You've got time! Isn't that nice? Like Lorrie Moore said: "Now you have time like warts on your hands. Slowly copy all of your friends' addresses into a new address book. Vacuum. Chew cough drops."

Boredom is fine. Read a lot of stuff that is impossibly good, maybe stuff you meant to read but never did. Take long walks with great music in your ears. Just don't do anything that's very distracting or engaging.

Let your thoughts about writing take over crazy amounts of real estate in your mind. It's a love affair, a very dangerous love affair.

3. I've got writer's block!

Many writers use alcohol, but you can try Adderall if you prefer. Ultimately, it doesn't matter. You don't even need to get intoxicated; most writers that I know don't. End of the day, you need to sit there and write sentences. Sentences tend to self-propagate through asexual reproduction like amoebas, so try writing a very bad sentence. Then another. Then another. Keep going until they're not bad. Once they're not bad, try to keep them that way. Finally, if writing is really that un-fun for you, you should quit and become a tax accountant. The world is in desperate need of tax accountants. The world does not need writers.

4. At (your age here), I'm too old to start now.

That Irish guy who wrote *Angela's Ashes*? Super old when he got on the horse the first time, like a hundred. Or sixty. Annie Proulx didn't really start writing fiction until she was in her forties, and things worked out pretty well for her. Deborah Eisenberg also started writing fiction in her late thirties and is crazily accomplished. She might also be immortal, however, because she's classy and ravishing and looks solidly middle-aged in person, but she's been publishing for decades, so . . . I'm just trying to do the math on this. Yeah, she's probably undead. Other examples abound. That fella Ben Fountain published his first novel recently, and he's a fossil. Margaret Atwood published her first novel at age thirty, which isn't that old, and actually she'd been an aspiring writer for half her life by then, but still . . .

5. My writing sucks.

That might be true. Welcome to the club! My first novel didn't sell, alas. No takers. I also didn't sell my second novel. Sent it around, but no takers. The reason they didn't sell was that they were fucking awful. I wrote, revised, and polished about thirty short stories, too, before I turned thirty.

Also finished those two novels by then. By the time of my thirtieth birthday, I had not received a single acceptance letter. Nada. Not one. The 1000 consecutive rejections I had received are in two boxes in my office.

At some point, my writing actually started improving. Maybe it was inevitable with that much practice. But I remember the moment it happened—there was a sharp line, before and after that moment. It was August 2005 on a beach in Ecuador and I was broke, had gone there because I knew a place that only charged $2 a night and I had a lot of air miles, so the ticket was free, and it was a whole lot cheaper than remaining in Seattle. These were meager times. I ate a lot of bread sandwiches. I was twenty-nine and a catastrophic failure in all things—or at least all the things I had so far attempted in life. But I started writing a story, and it was actually good, not in the fake way that I'd accidentally sneezed out a couple nice paragraphs before. This was actually good, the whole thing, it was like it was written by a real writer, like I was actually in control of these paragraphs. It was interesting, and vivid, and I was aware that there was a reader somewhere out there who would actually be interested in reading this. The reader might even pay to read it.

That was when I finally started to accept that readers don't inherently like you, they're not inclined to care about you and your goddamned life, and as a writer you must try to win them over with every single sentence. They're trying to watch *Breaking Bad*, which is understandable, and you're trying to convince them to stay and read the next sentence. It's a tug of war. You've got to try really hard, obviously. I fail all the time, still—in fact I fail most of the time—but since I figured that out, the vast majority of what I've written has found its way to publication.

6. Writing? I have a day job, so maybe when I retire.

No, actually there's a bus somewhere not far from you right now, and in fifteen months it's going to run you over. Sorry! It'll be really, really sad.

In any case, you have until then. Go get 'em, tiger!

7. But I have kids/a dog/a plant to take care of.

Yeah, dogs are not a good idea at all. Way too demanding. Very few writers have dogs, and very few writers have tattoos. It's a thing. I've got a complex theory about it that I'm going to write an essay about one day. Go to a writers' conference and ask around, you'll see what I mean— sure, some writers do have tattoos and dogs, just not very many. Get a cat. They won't need you so badly, and will at least look skeptical when you read aloud to them, just like a real editor.

Plants are fine, but get cheap ones so you won't feel bad when they die.

Kids are a problem, for sure. The gender expectations here are pretty bleak, favoring male autonomy (of course). But whatever your gender, it's kind of a motherfucking difficult thing. In the end, this is a big problem for writers, hence the divorce rate.

8. Choosing which or that? Everyone will laugh at my grammar/spelling.

Editors who acquire for publishing companies or magazines will not give more than one or, at most, two shits about your grammar/spelling. They'll like the way you write, what you have to say, or they won't. Once you're in, there are people on staff who can make you sound like you actually attended school.

9. My friends/literary community will mock my shit writing.

Probably not. If they do, they're assholes and you should make it your life's mission to destroy them and make them feel small. Hatred is one of the most invigorating emotions for an aspiring writer. Probably the best short story I've ever written was an attempt to "show them" in the most petty and childish way possible. I know it's not attractive! Sorry!! The story was published and anthologized. Later, a reader told me that she'd read it several times and it brought her to tears every time. I didn't ruin the moment by saying that I wrote the thing in a fit of vengeance toward people who'd doubted me.

10. I sent something in once and it was rejected.

Ha! That's so funny.

If a piece is rejected 30-40 times, maybe it should be sent to the special place where failed pieces of writing go, called Literature Valhalla, which is home to an extraordinary number of very good, even very, very good pieces of writing. Or you could just try again? Or you could re-write it and put a new title on it and try another 30-40 places.

It's a cliché, but it's very true: each failure is a step in the right direction.

As with most writers I know, I've had a piece rejected by a publi-cation somewhere and then, years later, I tried the same thing with the same place and it was accepted. *Oops!* Who knows why this happens? I have theories, but it doesn't really matter. I don't think about it too much. It doesn't do anything for you to think about it. In any case, the horse awaits you. Get back on that bastard and ride.

11. My friends or family will recognize themselves in the piece and sue/get mad at me.

Okay, here's my dubious advice on this score; please take it with a grain of salt. I think that only once the piece has been accepted for publication should you begin to think about this problem. You have some options:

a. Do nothing. Adios, motherfuckers! Personally, I've made quite a few enemies this way. It's sad for a while. Then it's not as sad any-more. Weigh the importance of the relationship against how much you want the piece to be in the world in the way that publication offers. Obviously, never admit that you did this.

b. If it's someone you like a lot, try begging forgiveness and/or insist that the piece is actually full of subtextual flattery. "Baby, it's about how awesome you are. I adore your honking laugh!"

c. If they're old, or the publication is regional, or if it's a literary magazine, try not showing it to the person in question. They will probably never hear about it.

d. No matter what, change names.

e. If it's worse than really bad, change names *and* ask an editor if they'll let you be anonymous. If not, maybe the piece gets moth-balled until that person who might be offended dies or becomes less important to you and you decide to cycle back to step A above.

12. All the Great Books have been written. There are no new stories out there.

In his loopy *Paris Review* interview, a presumably shitfaced William Faulkner said a lot of crazy and funny stuff. Some of it was also pretty astute, like how working as a landlord of a brothel is the ideal day job for an aspiring writer. But for the purpose of this question, I'll offer another nugget of wisdom from the same interview: "All of us failed to match our dream of perfection. So I rate us on the basis of our splendid failure to do the impossible . . . [An artist] believes each time that this time he will do it, bring it off. Of course he won't, which is why this condition is healthy. Once he did it, once he matched the work to the image, the dream, nothing would remain but to cut his throat, jump off the other side of that pinnacle of perfection into suicide. I'm a failed poet. Maybe every novelist wants to write poetry first, finds he can't, and then tries the short story, which is the most demanding form after poetry. And, failing at that, only then does he take up novel writing."

13. I'll start working on it as soon as I finish reading this book/ article on writing.

Books and articles about the writing life – including this one – mainly serve to reassure fellow writers that they are not alone. Writing is pretty fucking lonely, and it's easy to go crazy.

Writing about writing exists to say: "Buck up, chum, you're not so alone!" And: "If it's not working yet, just keep at it!" Sometimes it's a drill sergeant giving the advice, and sometimes the person is super smart, like Charles Baxter. But either way, that's what this is. It's like aspirin for the headache of years of struggling alone with sentences and the mountain of hard work without any reward. You're not going to learn how to write from reading these things. If you want to know how to be a better writer, go back to step one in this list.

How to Pirate a Treasure Chest
Ellaraine Lockie

Long before I became a professional poet/writer, I obsessively made notations of well-written sections or words that resonated in books I read, either underlining or listing word gems or phrases and their corresponding page numbers in the empty front pages of the books.

One summer I cleaned out my library but couldn't stand to get rid of any books that had those notations, so I started a binder that I call my Treasure Chest, where I listed every jeweled word that I recorded in the books.

The job was massive, as I'd never thrown away a book, not even the ones I'd marked *bad book*, for fear I'd forget and buy it again. The binder was thick, and gets thicker with nearly every book I read. Now, before beginning to read a book, I write its title and author's name on a blank, lined sheet of binder paper and place it in the back of the book. As I read, I list selected pearls of wisdom on the sheet with page numbers in case I want to quote or go back to the original source for context. If sections are longer than a short paragraph, I make a copy of the page, highlight the section and insert that in the binder.

The rewards consistently outsize the binder and the time and energy required by the process of creating it. Many times, an entire poem is inspired by one or two words on the list. For example, I read the phrase "cross over a crest" in a murder mystery while visiting New York City. The phrase joined my Treasure Chest list, and I quickly had a vision of the Montana where I grew up. It had been on my mind because so many New Yorkers seemed in awe of and a little apprehensive about this state inhabited by cowboys and Indians. Because many Montanans harbor similar feelings of awe and fear about New York City, I began imagining what a New Yorker might think and feel when visiting the Big Sky state. Hence the poem "First Time to Montana" wrote itself. Not only did the phrase "cross over a crest" inspire the poem, but it was also used in the poem.

Sometimes the Treasure Chest will help decide how to develop a particular subject into a poem. This was the case with a transformative experience I had during a stay in Montana—amazement and dilemma over a tree covered in the gold glitter of hundreds of dragonflies. I was contemplating a way into the poem and when skimming through the binder noticed the words, "fence of indecision," which gave me the foundation for the now published poem, "Photograph."

Even when I'm not actively writing, I can get a literary thrill from just reading the list out loud. The Treasure Chest is also a great solution for writer's block and an investment for the future when old age may prohibit travel or physical interaction with the world in ways that previously served to inspire writing.

You don't need to have a life-long stack of books with notations to compile a similar Treasure Chest. You can begin with what you're presently reading. If you're an avid reader, as most poets and writers are, you'll soon have a healthy list of writing prompts. Of course, the language and images in any given book are only as good as that author's writing skills. I've found, though, that even a mediocre book, say a vacation fast-read, can still have sections that are Treasure-Chest worthy.

I use a real binder and actual papers because I internalize better when I apply pen to paper and when I hold that same paper, as opposed to typing on a keyboard and reading from a computer screen. However, the process could be as successful in a computer file, especially if you read books electronically and can just scan the special sections into your designated file as you read the book. Either way, you can have a wealth of writing tools and inspiration at your fingertips to pirate your own Treasure Chest at any time.

First Time to Montana

The gravel road is rod straight
A car or pick-up truck every ten miles maybe
Square corners for turns
Nothing roundabout on the prairie
Dust plumes announce oncoming traffic
long before the driver waves a neighborly welcome
Whether or not you're a neighbor

You don't turn a corner or cross over a crest
to find towns tucked away
They greet you from fifteen miles away
Upfront like the people who inhabit them

Sagebrush scent seeps through the vent
from roadsides fringing wheat fields
That rotate with open range cattle
rolling tumbleweeds and antelope
that can keep up with cars
On a vastness that scares you
if you're an outsider
Someone who walks New York City streets
But has never seen mountains
from a flat mirage-like distance
Or pulled to the side of the road to pee
because the next service might be fifty miles

So you find yourself
pants down private parts exposed
Spellbound by the song of a meadowlark
The bluest and biggest sky
you've seen since *Out of Africa*

And a coyote pup crawling
from its hole twenty feet away
That you think you see
but can't quite comprehend

For sure you've forgotten any fear
of being scalped, shot or hung by vigilantes
The mother coyote comes to mind though
And breaks the spell so fast
you're back in the car
Before you notice your pants
still assembled around your ankles

Photograph

After a record rain, the first slice of sun
over the Bear Paw Mountains strikes a match
against a spruce by the cabin
An explosion of luminous gold encircles the tree
Alive in the swirl and low hum
Otherworldly in the prickles on my arm

Closer, the hum becomes a baby chainsaw buzz
operated by thousands of dragonflies
Their wings flapping 24-karat fluorescence
One worker lights on a finger
on hands folded in reverence

A live ring with four-inch wingspan of shimmer
that casts me onto the fence of indecision
Straddled between desire to own
or to honor a dragonfly's right to life

Its stereoscopic eyes look into mine
In them I see the necklace of ranch surrounding us
How it fits in the jigsaw puzzle of prairie
The species that crawl, jump, fly
swim, gallop, eat and mate before returning
to the soil to become food for the earth's survival

I see in these eyes how my shape must also fit
And I lean away from the fall
toward a cage or embalming fluid
Instead into the cabin
where a compromise waits
to capture the small miracle on my finger
To sanction the Jamaican belief
that a photo steals its subject's spirit

Nurturing Yourself and Your Writing Community: DIY Writing Retreats

Kara Provost

How do we keep our writing lives going? Between self-doubt, demands from work and home, feeling that there's already so much out there competing for our own and potential readers' attention, and the fact that no one bangs on our door clamoring for us to gift them with another poem or story, most of us find it challenging to carve out time and space for writing. As writers, we have to re-charge our own—and each other's—batteries, and help ourselves and our fellow writers refresh our creative wells. I have found making an annual DIY writing retreat a key source of support.

Remember those summer days when you were a kid and time just seemed to hang in the air like hazy sunlight? Why should the fun end when we grow up—why not create a writing vacation for yourself? About seven years ago, I made a tradition of setting aside time for some sort of writing retreat each summer, usually including one or two of my close writer or artist friends for co-inspiration. The DIY creative retreat doesn't have to be a big deal, especially if you have financial, family, and/or work constraints. I am fortunate to have a supportive partner, but even so, when my daughters were younger, I only went away for a weekend. It's amazing how just a couple days away from work, home, and family responsibilities can replenish your creative springs—and how much writing you can get done when you set apart a sacred time and space to write. (I once drafted twelve new poems during a five-day workshop at the Fine Arts Work Center in Provincetown, MA—by far a record for me!) A good writing retreat also fosters risk-taking. Getting out of your normal environment and habits loosens up the brain; take advantage of this during your writing retreat and push yourself to try new things.

Some suggestions for creating a DIY writing retreat:

- Find a friend or relative who has a vacation cabin, condo, or house, and trade your time or services for time away at their place. I have substitute-taught for a colleague at the college I work for in exchange for a couple days at her condo in Provincetown, for example.
- Split the cost of staying somewhere with a friend or two. Just be sure to choose wisely: pick someone who will give you space for writing, someone whose presence you find energizing or inspiring (or at least not distracting). If your friends are artists/writers themselves, all the better.
- Check into off-season rates at resorts, inns, or retreat centers. Hygeia House on Block Island (run by RI Poet Laureate Emeritus Lisa Starr) and Rolling Ridge Retreat Center in North Andover, MA (affiliated with the United Methodist Church, but open to anyone and not particularly churchy-feeling) are two options in New England. I've stayed at Rolling Ridge before, and it's both beautiful and inexpensive. You can share a room with a friend to cut down on cost—it used to be used as a summer camp, so you can even relive those slumber party experiences! You can also find numerous writing retreats, workshops, and writer-friendly houses or rooms to rent by looking at the websites or magazines for Poets and Writers (www.pw.org) or AWP (www.awpwriter.org).
- If you go away with a writer friend or two, have each of you bring some books you particularly like/are intrigued by and/or some writing handbooks with exercises in them to share—or make up prompts for each other to try. If you choose to retreat on your own, I still recommend bringing a few books that might help stimulate you to write, as well as some writing exercises to get the juices flowing.
- Sign up for an online writing workshop (or create your own with several other writers); do part or all of it from away

from home, staying someplace else or even just going out to
the library or coffee shop to escape all those other voices
and chores calling you.

What if you absolutely can't get away for a few days? Although it takes
more discipline, you can create a writing "staycation." Maybe take a week
or a few days off from work and set aside the bulk of your time for writing.
Be ruthless! In addition, or as an alternative to participating in an online
workshop during your DIY home retreat, try writing in new places or at
different times than you usually do; giving yourself assignments or writing
exercises; radically revising the form, genre, voice, length, etc. of a piece
you feel isn't working; and/or writing about topics or in forms or genres
you don't generally tackle.

If at all possible, I still recommend finding a way to leave home for
a writing retreat, even for just a couple of days. I have found them enormously worthwhile in terms of renewing my energy and commitment to
my creative work, nurturing my connections with the members of my
writing group who have participated with me, and increasing my creative
output. Start stashing away a little cash, saving up that vacation time, and
banking your family's goodwill—for your DIY writing retreat.

The Art of Breaking Hearts: Why I Write Fiction

Jason Kapcala

I have a confession to make. That mantra—"Fiction lies to convey the Truth"—I don't buy it. I realize that lying is a bad thing, and if we're going to dedicate an entire genre to it, we should have a good reason. It's just that every time I hear a writer use that cliché, I feel a little less connected to my own writing. I suppose it's because I don't have any Truths to tell—not in fiction, not in life.

One of my former teachers, Darrell Spencer, used to say that fiction "lies in order to wonder, and it speaks the voice of what it depicts." An acolyte of Chekhov, Darrell wasn't interested in sermonizing. When he sat down to write, all he wanted to do, he said, was "break a reader's heart." As with many of Darrell's teachings, I didn't understand what he meant at the time.

Darrell's lesson didn't sink in until years later. I had just arrived in West Virginia, and my new friend Jen asked to read something I had written, so I sent her a story about a couple dealing with the death of their child. I didn't know then what I know now—that Jen had lost a child herself. Had I known that, I would have sent her a different story. A few days after I emailed her my manuscript, Jen emailed me back and told me about her experience and how reading my story had made that loss feel fresh all over again. "It hurt to read," she said. "But it hurt in a good way. So I'm thanking you for writing it."

Reading that email, I started to understand what Darrell had been saying all those years ago. Nothing else I could have created would have caused that exact reaction from Jen—no picture I could have painted or song I could have sung or concerto I could have composed; it was the unique, slippery by-product of fiction, and it felt like the first important thing I'd ever done with my talents and my training. Now, I think of Jen and her experience every time I sit down to write.

Looking back, it's clear to me that I didn't teach my friend anything new by writing that story. I didn't sell her on the idea of redemption or instruct her on how to better live her life or show her how to deal with grief. There were no answers or epiphanies. And I didn't help my friend recover spiritually. In other words, there were no Truths conveyed by what I wrote.

I just followed a few characters that were important to me. I was curious about their world and empathetic about their struggle. I wondered how they would deal with their sudden tragedy, and I did my best to depict what I saw in my imagination. Through that act of following, I invited my friend to remember her own experiences, and I made her feel less lonely.

Perhaps that's what all good fiction does: remind us that we are not alone.

If you wanted to, you could subsume my anecdote under the umbrella of Truth. But for me, it points to a humbler phenomenon. Fiction writers lie—we fabricate characters, places, events—because it's our way of creating objects of beauty and setting them loose in the world. We do it hoping that someone will feel a connection to what we've written, and through that connection, we might just break that reader's heart.

The Secret and Successful Sentence
Melinda J. Combs

Contest points. Unreliable narrator. Point of view. Karaoke. Nudity. Monetary rewards. Basements or attics. My writing group, The Soggy Biscuits, has utilized all of these as writing inspiration. Some have worked. Some haven't. Luckily, the nudity needed to be included in the writing. When we had to write with an unreliable narrator, I reread Robert Olen Butler's "Jealous Husband Returns in Form of Parrot" and wrote about a character who goes crazy over a half-dressed mannequin in a store window. When a scene had to occur in a basement or attic, we all generated dark, troubling stories.

For a quick background, we have seven Soggy Biscuits. Eric, Jenn, Garrett, and John are the novelists in the group while Jeff writes mostly satires and Abbe is a playwright/screenwriter. I'm finishing a memoir and starting a screenplay. In between our major projects, we all write short stories. At the end of our monthly meetings, we brainstorm exercises and this one has proven the most fruitful: we each write the first sentence of a story and then submit it to Eric, who then redistributes the sentences without the author's name attached.

Once Eric has collected every Biscuit's sentence, he divvies them out. Sometimes, he tries to match authors with sentences that tend to be in their wheel house. But, "most of the time I try to match authors with sentences that say to me 'this person would never write a sentence like this' just to see what they will do with it."

What we do with these sentences is where the greatness occurs. These exercises have given me the opportunity to write in completely new ways: from a male perspective, about a seven-sided die (I had to Google it before I started), and with a historical event about fictitious characters.

When I received "The trees — all Pinus lambertiana, he believed — were bent at a dangerous angle by a dominatrix wind, ready to fall on his head and humiliate him," I focused on writing about a character battling his fear of objects falling on his head. I created George, whose life is run by numbers and exactitudes and who as a child saw a program about a dirigible crashing into a bank building, which led to his fear. I decided on the fear sparked by a TV show because, when I was young, I watched a documentary in which a woman's leg is bitten off by a shark. That has stuck with me and given me my greatest fear, so I wanted George to have a similar experience. Then, I worked to include adjectives that parallel "dominatrix wind," because that part of the sentence resonated with me the most. So, I incorporated "sanguine Monday," "oscillating eight years" and "tippy Cocos Nucifera." Because I often forget to include adjectives, this gave me the chance to use them precisely and deliberately. That one sentence has blossomed into a funny, voice-driven, ten-page piece that I'm proud of.

John, our most literary Biscuit, was assigned this first sentence: "It's already fuck ugly, so just walk on by, he told himself, keeping his gaze upon his feet and drawing six breaths in time with his footsteps, but losing his shit on the seventh breath when one of the little punks pelted the statue again, this time with a fucking holotag of all things." For his entry, John focused on 'holotag': "I don't write sci-fi, so it was a challenge for me to create that kind of universe. When I googled 'holotag' I found no such item existed, which was much better because I had the freedom to make something up." With the story in publishable shape, John has submitted it to a few science fiction journals — something he's never done before nor anticipated he ever would.

When I read my most recently assigned sentence, I was stumped: "This time it was cars in my dream, hurled up a mile into the air — hundreds of them, spewing up and around like a rainbird sprinkler, careening first into the distant landscape, and then ever closer, and finally into the crowds of people fleeing in terror around me." I've never written about a car accident nor would I think to do so. But I researched famous car crashes and decided to describe the 1955 Le Mans accident from the point of view of a son who attended the race with his father. It's modeled after Jim Shepard's story, "Love and Hydrogen," which is about two gay characters on board the doomed Hindenburg crash in 1937. My fiction tends to lean toward fabulist (wife turns husband into a fork), so to entwine fact and fiction opens up a different realm of possibilities I'm eager to pursue.

Now, as the exercise is six months in, the Biscuits disguise their voices and make the sentences more challenging — not only for the writer but for themselves. John has developed methodologies in writing the first sentence. He tries to establish a world: "Sometimes I do that through made-up language ('shnazzies' and 'bitties'), or through a contradiction (the enfant terrible of the harp world) or through an unusual character ('She started licking things.')." For me, I want to submit a first sentence that is challenging and unexpected, so, for my very first sentence, I submitted an equation since I've never seen one open a story: "If X plus Y equals Z, and A plus B equals C, then Z plus C equals 27." Jenn, who usually writes about characters obsessed with an art, like cake decorating or piano playing, was initially tormented by this assignment, but she produced a noir story about a drug deal gone wrong with a tough, gritty voice and the darkest characters she's ever written.

This exercise also works well because it eliminates the intimidation of the blank screen, which has hung all of us up in the past, particularly Jeff, as he's recovering from a long bout of writer's block: "These little starter sentences are a creative kick in the pants. All I have to do is pick up the idea and run with it — in whichever direction suits my imagination. There's real freedom in that."

None of us expected this exercise to make us so prolific, but it has. We're innovative, challenged, and even a bit sneaky (some of us try to take on another Biscuit's typical voice to throw off the recipient). Part of the fun of this exercise is not knowing who wrote the first sentence. Of course, there's guessing, but the writer can't reveal him or herself until after the piece is workshopped. There's also a sense of collaboration which softens the isolation of writing and which creates even more excitement in reading everyone's work (Who has my sentence? What did they do with it?). But because there is a sense of obligation for all of us — we don't want to let down the author of the original sentence — everyone completes this assignment. We get our butts in the chair and produce new, unexpected writing, which shows us that we are growing into better, stronger, and more versatile writers — and all because of somebody else's first sentence.

Deep Breaths and Small Stones: Haiku as a Tool for Writer's Block

Allyson Whipple

World like a dewdrop
though it's only a dewdrop
even so, even so.

There is no shortage of discussion about the dreaded writer's block in the writing community. Whether you write poetry, pulp novels, biographies, or any other form or genre, there will be talk of blocks, what causes them, and how to fix them. Different writers and teachers will come up with different strategies. Stream of consciousness exercises; working in new genres; switching projects; getting exercise. Some suggest the less-healthy options of massive amounts of caffeine or alcohol.

One of the most commonly repeated pearls of advice I see is to keep writing. Whether it's through exercises, different projects, or simply sitting down and forcing your pen to move across the page, the most important thing seems to be that you sit down and get words out. They don't have to be good words. They don't have to be publishable. They just have to be words that get out of your hands and your head. And eventually, through dogged persistence, the block will dissolve.

Sometimes, though, even the idea of writing through it can be daunting. Switching genres or projects can be scary. The thought of sitting down and forcing the words out can seem exhausting before you even begin. And this fear, or this fatigue, can prevent you from even trying, which can make the block worse.

When I feel this way, when I feel worn out at the thought of even trying—this is when I turn to my haiku practice. More than anything else, it sustains me through periods when I'm blocked. When it comes to my writing, the haiku form is not just a way to get words out when I'm stuck; the practice of haiku itself lends itself to becoming present, and through that presence, shaking off the distractions that block you.

Wait! Don't strike that fly!
he's wringing his hands there
and wringing his feet.

Haiku is not really about *writing*. It is about *stillness, presence,* and *observation*. It is about engagement with the world around you. It gets you away from the computer giving you eyestrain, the page that intimidates you by its blankness. It takes you away from the environment that stifles you, and takes you out into the world.

You will find books and articles and blog posts with instructions for how to write haiku. There will be notes about using a syllabic pattern of 5/7/5. There will be other instructions saying to disregard the 5/7/5 structure. You may or may not be told to include a seasonal reference. You may be told to write the entire haiku as one line, or in three lines. And that the middle line should be the longest.

But what you really need in order to write haiku is simply a comfortable place to sit. Outdoors is preferable. If that's not possible, somewhere with a big, clean window. You might find haiku in your kitchen or your living room, but you'll find more activity, engagement, and refreshment by getting out. And you don't have to have a big backyard or live in the country. Urban environments lend themselves just as well to haiku, because haiku is not about where you are—it's about what you see.

When you go to write your haiku, you should have a pen and paper, but I don't recommend keeping them in front of you. Keep them in your pocket or your purse. Know they're available, but don't take them out and act as though they are an expectation. They only need to come out when you are ready.

And then—sit. Just sit, and observe. And when you observe a moment that you find worthy of haiku, write that haiku. And then you have put down words, which is what you've been advised to do to beat writer's block.

Have you written many words? No. But it's not about quantity. It's about harnessing a moment that you find beautiful or poignant or essential, and putting it on paper. Isn't that what writing is really all about?

The best thing about haiku is that you don't have to think, really. Writer's block is about a lack of ideas, a struggle with thoughts. But haiku is not about having good or bad ideas. It's not about logic or intellect. It is about sitting in the present and *seeing* what is necessary rather than ruminating about it.

And if you sit for a whole afternoon and don't find anything you want to write a haiku about? That's okay. You've still committed yourself to being present with your surroundings. And even if you haven't written a single line on that page, you've still done work to combat writer's block. Because while writing words is important, so is disengaging from the sources of your stress and *re-engaging* with the world around you. And if you sit in the world, if you observe it, even if you don't commit any of it to paper, you have still been present. You have distanced yourself from your troubles and cleared your head. So perhaps tomorrow, when you try to work on your next book or story, you will in fact have come unblocked.

> *The radish puller*
> *pointing with a radish root*
> *teaches me the way.*

And all those rules I mentioned before? The ones I told you not to worry about? You can use them if you want. If writing in 5/7/5 helps you focus, helps you get through that block, go for it. If you prefer to use a twelve or seventeen-syllable total rather than focusing on specific line syllables, that's great. If keeping your haiku in three lines every time provides benefit to your mind and your writing, use three lines. Does a seasonal reference help ground you? Then by all means, use one!

But if not? If you just want to write down an impression without worrying about syllables or lines or seasons? Then go for it. Haiku have formal constraints, and some people find these constraints to be a boon to their creativity. But because forms evolve, and because certain formal rules don't translate easily from Japanese to English (or other languages), you can feel free to change things around, to create a haiku that works for you. Because your presence in the world is more important than your poetic form.

And if for some reason you don't want to use formal constraints, but feel uncomfortable calling what you produce a haiku, you don't have to call it that. You could refer to it as a poem or a fragment. Two Buddhist writers in England, Satya Robin and Kaspalita of the Writing Our Way Home site, use the term *small stones* for pieces of writing that don't follow the conventions of haiku or other brief poems but are written in the spirit of mindfulness and presence.

> *Smokes the waterfall*
> *and even seen close at hand*
> *the cherry flowers are clouds.*

Haiku even work well for those who find the isolation of writing to be the biggest cause of blockage. It is not just a practice to be undertaken in isolation, away from others. Haiku circles are a way to practice mindful writing in a more social setting. Granted, a haiku circle is not the kind of place where you go to chit-chat about that difficult plot hole in your mystery novel, or the struggles you have revising your new poetry collection. Rather, it is a supportive, reflective space to sit, write, and share.

Renga circles are another way for writers to practice mindful writing and become unblocked in a social setting. Whereas a haiku circle is focused on passing around haiku, writing down the ones that resonate with you, and sharing them, renga circles are about building one collaborative piece. Like haiku, renga have some formal constraints, but in your own circle, practicing your own mindfulness, you should feel free to adjust the rules to suit the needs of your group.

> *The mountain crumbles*
> *and with a look of unconcern*
> *up rises a snipe.*

When practiced regularly, haiku (or other forms of mindful writing) can free you from blockage, but can also help to keep stagnation at bay. When even a small portion of your day is focused on attention and presence, when you make mindfulness a habit, you just might find that when the time comes to return to your computer or notebook, you'll already be refreshed and ready to go. And even if blockage returns, you'll also know that there is a way out.

Perhaps the best thing about using haiku as a tool for writer's block is that you don't need special training in it. You don't need to be a poet. You don't need to have anything published. You don't need to have an MFA. It is a mindfulness practice that suits all writers at all stages of their careers.

Note: All haiku used in this article were written by Issa (1763-1827).

Of Constancy
Nicole Walker

The Peripatetic sage does not exempt himself totally from perturbations of mind, but he moderates them.

—Montaigne

Emeritus marketing professor Theodore Leavitt lectured to his students, "The reason the train industry could not compete with the automobile industry was because it failed to recognize that it was not in the *railroad* industry but in the *transportation* industry [emphasis mine]." But how can you expect the train industry to forego its iron beginnings? The heavier the rails, the faster the train—that was how it worked then. It's the opposite thought to current-day, feather-weight travel. Fiberglass and super light aluminum—that's the domain of the transportation industry. The train industry knows what it's good at. Ruts. Lines. Permanence.

An online, less-reputable-than-the-OED etymology website says that "rut" means "narrow track worn or cut in the ground." First used in the 1570s, probably taken from the Middle English word for route. However, the OED finds this "improbable." But perhaps it is the OED that is in a rut.

Every day I wake up at 6:55. I make my kids' lunch: pepperoni, rice, yogurt, grapes, pretzels, carrots, juice. I eat an English muffin, then check Facebook, Gmail, work email. Then I check work email, Gmail, and Facebook. I grade student essay one, check email, essay two, check Gmail, essay three, Facebook, essay four. I hold office hours. I tell students that their Spanish courses will fulfill their cultural understanding block. I teach. I tell students that the difference between dissociation and distance in a narrator is how willing the narrator is to be obviously broken. It is better to be broken. You can see yourself better, like when the bone of an arm breaks through the skin and for the first time ever you see your inside, now out.

I come home. I make dinner—tacos. I have a glass of wine. I watch a show called TV. I go to bed at 10. I wake up at 6:55.

I am in a rut but it's okay because I'm a lover of routine. No disrespect to the OED, but I love my route. A well-worn route is a rut. A well-worn routine is a life capable of heavy lifting. You can do the work of a thousand boxcars. You are iron track, trains running along the back of you. A rut-lover is a conveyer of speed. My life is going so quickly. My rails are on fire.

People, like my husband Erik or his parents, try to convince me to travel. I'm conflicted. I want to go—Napa sounds beautiful. I like wine. I don't want to go. It's far away. I'd have to take an airplane. It will disrupt my route. A self, divided. My father-in-law sets up the trip. Three days of wine drinking at Far Niente, Chateau Montelena, Caymus. "We'll get the rooms," he said. "You just have to buy your plane tickets and the wine tastings." $99 companion tickets. $99 a tasting. $99 a dinner. The transportation industry is not always a bargain but $297 is not bad for three day vacation.

We forgot, Erik and I, in our calculations, to include the cost of traffic. It took us three hours to drive fifty-five miles. That night, a tangle of stop-and-go nerves, I lay awake in bed. Too much wine and a too fluffy pillow triggered trains of thoughts: the flight attendant's eyebrows, the waiter's glasses, the definition of "tasting," plastic water bottles, recyclable or not, the surreptitious reuse of other people's water bottles, contagion, the avian flu, flu shots versus flu mist, wondering if I am a bad parent to say okay to flu mist for one child, a shot for the other, and if I, that same bad parent who left her kids with a babysitter, who is not sleeping in the middle of Napa, sated and spoiled and a little bit drunk, should give up and get up.

I go outside. The vineyards layer in rows. The bad parent walks between the vines at five in the morning. It is fall and the leaves of the Cabernet turn yellow like the leaves at home in Flagstaff. I take some comfort in this—I am missing red leaves equally, everywhere— although comfort is not the same as sleep.

In the 1940's, National City Lines, a front company for General Motors, began dismantling light-rail based trolley lines in big cities. Called the GM Streetcar conspiracy, the rigid rail lines were replaced with flexible, bendable, turnable, car-able roads. No longer did the city worker have to abide by the strict rules of pre-determined tracks. If the worker wanted to take A Street to work, he took A Street. If he wanted Lexington, he took Lex. If he wanted to turn around and go home, he could circle that car in the middle of any intersection, at least in Utah where the U in Utah means freedom to go in circles on wide streets forevermore, thy will is thy command.

I'd rather drive than fly. Driving is more familiar. I do it every day. My car is nicely beige—a color as comforting as sand. If I am driving, I can stop to pee at any convenient Shell station along the way. I try not to stop at Texaco because if there's one constancy in my life, it's a prejudice against Texas. The other constancy, because constancies should multiply, is the persistent belief that Shell oil comes from kinder oil places than Texas. I shouldn't drive or fly at all. Global warming. Perhaps I should take the train, except Amtrak is the only game in town. They must give way to freight trains. It takes forever to go fifty-five miles on Amtrak. Freight trains are as numerous as prejudices and interruptions. Perhaps, instead, I will stay home.

Like prejudices and interruptions, ton-miles add up. In the US, in 1975, freight trains carried 750 billion ton-miles of freight. By 2005, that amount had doubled. Ton-miles by rail release far less carbon than those by car or plane: 43 kilograms per five hundred miles versus 103 for a small car, 207 for a large car, and 137.9 for a plane. The plane is the most dangerous, both to the routine and to the air. When I am on the plane, I need to sit in the aisle. If I don't sit in the aisle, I weep. Mostly for my bladder. Sometimes from my bladder. If there's one thing I must do, it is to feel free to pee on a regular basis.

Unilaterally, my friend Rebecca won't fly. In 2010, she took the train from Los Angeles to New York City for her art opening at Ameriger Yohe. She boarded the train at 10 p.m. Having booked a bedroom, she unpacked her pants, her shirts, her dress, her books. Bedrooms are for two and she was traveling alone. Plenty of room to make herself at home. Plenty of time, too. It would take three days to cross the country. Three days if all went well. Time enough to establish a routine.

To take the 4 Southwest Chief from LA through Flagstaff, through Albuquerque onward to Chicago, takes forty-four hours and costs $1,931. Then you still have to transfer to, and pay for, the 48 Lake Shore from Chicago to Albany to New York City. At five o'clock that evening she called me. She had made it only five-hundred miles in nineteen hours. I was in downtown Flagstaff, walking through the square after dinner at Karma Sushi's. We always walk around the block after dinner at Karma's. We stop at Mountain Sports and Aspen Sports and Babbitt's to look at NorthFace and Patagonia gear that we never buy. Max, my son, tries on a hat that reads, Life is Good. Zoe, my daughter, asks if she can have flashlight shaped like an iguana. Rebecca calls me. She's in the station. I wave to her through the walls of the store, across Route 66, through the metal of the sleeping car. She can't get off to say hello. There has been a delay. A woman walked in front of the train. The train could not, as it never can, stop in time. I tell her, they do that, in Flagstaff. Walk in front of trains. I picture the woman, long blue coat, hair flying out behind her. I picture her pushing a stroller away from her. I don't know if there is a stroller but I see one. Maybe in my imagination, she's pushing her better self away. Maybe she's wishing that she could send the happy part of her to go on and on while the unhappy part could be stopped by the poor train conductor's heavy load. What a great human achievement, even surpassing the invention of the transportation industry, to divide routine from despair.

But Rebecca is stuck with both routine and despair and is thus stuck on that train and there is no way around if she wants to make it to Chicago.

She waited so patiently, since patient is the only thing you can be on a train that goes only one direction on tracks that turn only toward Chicago. Despite her patience, she missed the transfer. To make the show on time, she was forced to take a plane. O'Hare to LaGuardia in an hour and a half. An hour and a half to defy death. To withstand the unnaturalness of flight. To put the fear that you're tearing through God's cloak of safety in same compartment away from you. Now she's done it. She's changed her mind. Her policy. Her beliefs. To change your mind is to kill your former self. Rebecca is anything but suicidal and yet, here she is, torn in two, half on the train, half in New York City.

I am suicidal. All my friends are dead. Or dying. Or will be dead one day. My husband, when I said that I couldn't go on, thought I said, "Do you want chicken for dinner?" I didn't correct him but the poor chicken is dead too. My husband kisses the top of my head. Internal, eternal war: There is purpose in death but better purpose in dinner. I will make fried chicken, chicken cacciatore, chicken fricassee, chicken and dumplings, chicken tacos, chicken in a can. There is purpose in life again. Then, the chicken burns. I want to die. I turn on the radio to hear Maggotbrain's "Can You Get to That?" They sing, "You're going to reap just what you sow." Sow: My daughter and son swing together in concert. There is order and balance in the universe. Life is good and even.

Reap. My daughter, older, jumps off the swing, sticks the landing. My son, before I can stop him, follows suit. He falls to the ground. Cracks his chin open. I should have stopped him, should have stopped them. I have no power. There is no justice. I sowed. He reaped. I remain resolved. I will live. I will die. From the cherry tree, the blossoms fly off into summer heat. They count one more day, one more day. I have never been so happy to be alive. So sad. I shall fight myself no more forever.

What would Professor Emeritus Leavitt have had the railroad industry do? What does he mean they failed to realize what industry they were in? Who is the *they* here? Robber Barons? Getty? Rockefellers? Monopoly? Henry Ford? Does Leavitt mean the railroad industry should have started building cars, divided themselves in two? Should have expanded to absorb all transportation—automobile, aeronautical. The trains should have become cars? Or should they have become more themselves? Is there a way the railroad industry could have kept the trains or the tracks? Is there an America that could have been tracked, where the individual would not want to make his left turn at will, her U-turn at random? Could America have been America crisscrossed by railroad rather than held up high by overpasses and bridges? The railroad industry failed to become the automobile industry. Adapt. The times. The fossil fuels will be gone soon. Use them while you can. We seem to be willing to abide the plane that goes only to the stops already determined, sometimes making us wait for hours to layover some place we distinctly do not want to be. We recover by getting off the plane and quickly finding a taxicab, a Town Car, our mother in her Prius to pick us up at the curb. The train speeds by, empty.

I love my routine of hours but I hate the routine of morning. Same soap. Same contact lenses. Same hair brush I bought in Portland, Oregon's Aveda when I was pregnant with my daughter and traveling for the first time to read to students—at Evergreen State. I was pregnant with the new. Traveling didn't seem so hard then, even though I slept on a cot at my friend's house in Portland. Even though I was put in my host's bedroom, in a bed so redolent with graciousness (who can sleep in their host's beds while the hosts sleep on the fold out?). I slept. Everything was a first time and I crashed into it. Life was a bucket of sleep and I soaked in it but now my pants are so old and my shirts are so old and I'm tired of drying the water off from behind my knees. This face I've looked at before with these old eyes and the old thoughts are dull as a doorknob. I don't want to die. I want a new brain. A neural net with pathways ungrooved. I want some new pants.

The war with the self is the most brutal war. Is there anything more heavy than the re-collection of track by the industry that laid them down? Railroad ties resold at the local nursery as landscaping tools. Spikes melted down into wheelbarrows. Tracks themselves pressed into service as dumpsters and graffiti canvas. A railroad industry cannibalized by a transportation industry. Pulling up tracks is sentimental. Can you turn old business into a new garden?

After the latest oil crisis, after Iran, Iraq, Syria, Hurricane Katrina and the Gulf Oil Spill—after the world continued to be its inconstant self—gas prices rose so high that it became less expensive to ship freight by train than by semi-trailer. Stopped at the crossing, as I check my email, Facebook, Gmail, brush my hair, the box cars flash by as do flatbed cars topped with trailers normally attached to semi-trucks. Boxcar after boxcar speeds by. Rubber-tired-trailers filled with freight one gasoline fed engine at a time bounce on top of steel wheels, going forward, mostly gas-free. Maybe there was forethought. Or slow thought.

The railroad industry is doing fine. They say they're going to build a train from L.A. to Napa. It's a straight shot. Save a lot of gas. Someone in the railroad industry in an industry that doubles as the transportation industry chose that straight line because taking every available turn sometimes gets you nowhere, especially in California, where no one ever wants to die, unless they're trapped in traffic.

Here's a new thought for another trap: Roads are asphalt train tracks. You're still driving where someone else is telling you to go. A new neural net can't be paved. How do you make a new thought? You have to move. It's worse than travel, I know. The packing and the goodbye saying and the finding a new grocery store. But you have to go. The tulips you see in Michigan are not the same tulips you see in Phoenix. That tulip, eaten by a javelina, will break your mind. Inside that broken mind, on the edge of a gnawed tulip, you will find a reason to live. It's called yellow. You have never seen a yellow like this before. Keep looking at it until you have to move again.

Or maybe you have never seen a tulip. Maybe you should get out of your car. Leave it by the jangling railroad stop. The noise will go away soon enough. The other cars will find you. You'll be surprised how smooth the ground next to the tracks is. Don't worry. You won't trip. The tracks are dangerous but the weeds alongside never are. It's a route that's been taken a million times but never once by you. You might think its suicide for a flower to grow along this route—from Flagstaff to Los Angeles is mostly Mojave. But the Utah Penstemon grows there. You're from Utah. It survives. So can you. Indian paintbrush survives everywhere, even here, in between the oil-dipped lumber and the steel spikes, between the Turtle Mountain Wilderness and Barstow. You are willing to take note. You take comfort in color. Even Desert Dandelion seems surprising, in the desert, even though it looks as routine as the ones stuck in your hard dirt at home. Desert Larkspur is as blue as your coat and Owl's Clover is pink for the owl that is calling you to go ahead. This rut is less of a route. You're going so slow you might actually get somewhere.

Advice to Mary Ellen Miller's Poetry Writing Class

John Guzlowski

First, listen carefully to the advice of older poets, like me.
Some of what they say will be the most important thing
you'll hear about poetry. Some of what they say
will be useless. How can you tell the difference?
You can't right now, but you will in five or ten years.

Second, find someone who believes in your poetry,
a wife, a lover, a friend, and believe what they say
about your poetry, the good and the bad both,
and keep writing, writing all the time, writing emails,
letters, notes on the backs of books, term papers
about Dostoevsky and the rise of realism, write jokes
about mules that speak only French and teachers
that wear red ties and white wide-brimmed hats,
and writing like this, you'll find you're writing poems,
all the time, everyday, everywhere you're writing poems.

Third, write a poem everyday, and if you can't write one
everyday write one every other day, and if you can't do that
write one every third day, and if you can't do that
write one when the muse hits you—when two words
explode in your head, appear from out of nowhere.
Whatever you're doing when that explosion hits,
stop, and write down the sound of that explosion
because if you wait 'til later it's lost—absolutely.

Fourth, find a muse. I'm not kidding. Mine is a mother
of two who died in the snow outside of Stalingrad,
shot in the forehead by a German foot soldier
from a little town in Bavaria. She comes to me
when I'm busy grading papers or talking with friends
and she begs me to remember her children, all the children.

What will this muse do for you? Ask her, she'll tell you.

Ritual and the Symbiotic Magic of Yoga and Writing

Jessica Reidy

We hear that writers are crazy and miserable people. I don't necessarily mean crazy in the clinical, mental illness sort of way, though sometimes we are that too. "Writer crazy" is that unspecified, wild-eyed, solitary unhappiness exalted and romanticized in films, books, television, plays, songs, because what could be more romantic than the manic sadness of a tragic visionary who collapses under her own magnificent world? It's a blessing and a curse. Meanwhile, my friends who are doctors, therapists, and psychologists vehemently assure me that artists who struggle with mental illness are usually less productive or entirely unproductive in periods of illness compared to their periods of stability, wellness, or recovery. While instability and isolation do not support sustained prolific creativity, fortunately, the road to "You can get it!" is paved with easily accessible self-care and support. It's a matter of finding the practices and communities that support you.

Many practices that you can do on your own, at home, and for free or for rather cheap can beautifully maintain a creative writer's balance and feed her craft: yoga, meditation, journaling, mandala coloring, breathing exercises, running, swimming, riding, long walks or hikes in nature…Whatever it is, it's important that the activity is performed with awareness, mindfulness, and an engagement with the present moment. It should render your mind a quiet, fertile place. *Ritual* feels like the perfect word for the act of cultivating a nourishing writing practice—what you do to prepare for (or complement) writing should be a kind of dedication with mental, physical, and emotional signals that communicate to your mind and body that it's time to create.

I find that yoga is everything. Simply, the more I practice yoga, meditation, exercise, and clean eating, the more energy I have to write, the more I want to create, the more I create, the more I feel at home in the world.

When I prepare myself for writing by centering in a quiet meditation with mindful *pranayama* (breathing practices), setting an intention to create, and preparing my body with asana (yoga postures), I have constant, spontaneous epiphanies and ideas about my novel-in-progress that actually go somewhere, and often arrive alongside healing realizations about my own happiness and history.

You may have heard of "yoga off the mat," the practice of living being present, mindful, and loving and following the path of *ahimsa* (non-violence) in your everyday life and not just in yoga class. Yoga is guided by the breath—the breath is what grounds your experience, paces movement, sends *prana* (life force) through the body, awakens the brain, relaxes the muscles, and soothes the nervous system. It is your constant companion—it arrived with you when you were born and will leave with you when you die. Consider how many of our breaths we miss—how many hurried, scanty breaths we take. Even when our body is crying out for oxygen, even when anxiety or anger rears, we still forget that controlling our breath is controlling our bodies. When you slow and deepen your breathing, it sends a signal to your brain that you are safe. Your heartbeat slows, adrenaline stops pumping, and you return to the present moment on the back of your breath. Even the simple intention to be present with your breath throughout the day will root you in your experience.

The intention of embodied awareness, being present, is a worthy one, especially for an artist. Robert Olen Butler, Pulitzer Prize winner and author of The Christopher Marlowe Cobb Thriller Series, argues that ritual is the key to creating art. In *From Where You Dream: the process of writing fiction*, he explains that you must prepare for writing by entering a trance and focusing on the breath in a quiet space, much like the centering meditation of a yoga class. Once you're there and centered, you must stay present with sensation and allow yourself to create directly and organically from that "dream space." Like in yoga, you set an intention to stay open to all experience and at the same time, remain unattached to ideas, hence the popular mantra, "I am not my mind." Butler writes that the best art comes from this "moment to moment sensual experience," and "non-art" is full of summarized or intellectualized reported experience.

Those "moment to moment sensory experience[s]" are much more nuanced than you'd think—all the available senses are involved. In my Yoga Teacher Training at Kripalu, I learned that the body holds memories, a phenomenon addressed in the study of *somatics*, a branch of psychology that examines the mind-body connection. In certain poses, you may feel spontaneously happy, sad, angry, frightened, blissful—you may be flooded with memories, sensations, and epiphanies. You may weep or laugh without knowing why (or knowing all too well why). Stay with the present if you can: breathe, relax, feel, watch, allow (BRFWA). Your body is releasing trapped energy, memories, and emotions—parts of your past that you have been carrying unconsciously, perhaps as tension, shortness of breath, pain, or anxiety. What does the experience feel like, smell like, look like, sound like, and taste like? The information you need to have a cathartic experience is the same information you need to create one on the page. Butler argues that in order to make art, we have to dive into the unconscious mind, confront whatever pain dwells there, and use that intense awareness to write from the "white hot center." This is just another way to access the unconscious.

That's why *asana* are good practice for writing and vice versa. *Asana* comprise a moving meditation that deepens the trance and simultaneously directs awareness inside and outside the body so that one experiences the world fully without translating sensation and impression into ideas. Now I keep a notebook and pen beside my mat so I can jot down notes and phrases that feel organic, and likewise, I keep a mat by my writing space so I can explore sensation when I feel stuck. Originally, the asana component of yoga was developed to prepare the body to comfortably sustain sitting meditation, which may as well be a writing session. Writer Natalie Goldberg draws on her experience studying sitting meditation with Zen Master Roshi in her craft guide *Writing Down the Bones*. Her writing exercises and advice are a natural extension of Zen meditation, focusing on mindfulness, acceptance, and quieting the "monkey mind," a Buddhist and Hindu term for a mind that chatters with endless distractions (sounds familiar). She currently leads workshops and writing retreats using this meditative approach to writing. You can practice conjuring up creativity through breathing exercises, postures, chants, mudras (ritual symbols or gestures), meditation, and yogic philosophy. Play consciously with the kinship between practicing yoga and practicing art.

In her book *The Artist's Way*, creativity guru Julia Cameron encourages both engaging with the unconscious and play. For tapping into the unconscious, she swears by stream-of-consciousness journaling first thing in the morning every day, no matter your art or craft. She calls these three pages of automatic writing "morning pages," and they are intended to be a judgment-free space for you to blurt out all the garbage in your brain, find relief, and safely brainstorm new ideas that might seem too fragile or risky to commit to paper otherwise. The idea is, if you express your crazy and make yourself aware of it before you begin making your day's art, you are clear-headed enough to get down to business. And for play, she suggests weekly solo "artist dates" to cultivate play and creativity—it could be anything from a trip to the craft store for some stickers for your notebook or a lovely walk along the river.

Cameron firmly believes that artists needn't be crazy or miserable, and acknowledges that being a happy artist takes work and maintenance, especially since there is some truth behind the crazy writer stereotype: job uncertainty, delusions of fame and failure, battling the ego, cutthroat competition, and constantly having to justify 'impractical' life choices to other, more 'stable' friends, family, and nosy strangers. All of these are difficult to cope with on their own terms. Then there's the extraordinarily demanding amount of introspection that artists and writers have to engage in to try and understand the human condition. As artists, we need sword-sharp analytical and interpretative skills, and we risk getting the sword stuck in our ribs. And yet, we must engage in some of this painful introspection in order to create something meaningful. By *meaningful*, I mean what Erin Belieu, powerhouse poet and co-founder of VIDA: Women in Literary Arts, means when she tells her students to write something "true and surprising." She says, "Tell me something I know, not something I *already* know." Cameron's workbook is intended to guide you through the work of overcoming creativity blockages and confronting any conscious or subconscious negative ideas about your ability and right to create and to listen deeply to the "child-self" for in-spiration and affirmation. There's a lot of play and love in her method, but it is ritualized play and love. The affirmations, morning pages, artist dates, creative tasks, and all the rest are daily or at least weekly events. And you've got to admit, there's something beautiful about starting your work with a ritual of love and play.

And here comes the yoga love. One of my biggest struggles with yoga is the "unconditional love for all beings" business, which is essen-tial to yoga and writing, and probably key to happiness and eternal bliss. Loving your loved ones is easy, but loving yourself is hard, especially if, like most people, you've been through abuse and struggle with shame, self-loathing, and its variants. But you need to try. Love all of your first attempts for what they are. Embrace what yogis call "beginner's mind," and what writer Anne Lamott calls "shitty first drafts." Let things be bad at first because they will get better, but they need room to breathe. And when it's time to show your work to someone, look for writer friends you can trust to look at your messy, fragile baby bird novel, as ugly and wet as it is, and to not smash it into the ground.

Instead, they'll give you advice to help it grow up into some more presentable stage of bird. Yoga asks the practitioner to sacrifice her ego, just as the writer must surrender her ego in order to allow herself the space to draft and try out those imperfect ideas. (Or lay those imperfect eggs? I don't want to stretch this metaphor too much.)

And while love for the rest of the world, all the lovely people and neutral people, isn't so hard to imagine, love for all the murderers, rapists, child abusers, puppy-kickers, and Bill O'Reilly is much more challenging. It hurts me to imagine loving them, but the intention of unconditional love is the North Star to a life of *ahimsa*, and the pain points to areas that are still tender in my life. Those white hot centers. Love for all beings also kindles a writer's ability to empathize with and understand every possible charac-ter, no matter how terrible, wonderful, or strange their (or your) actions may be, and love them despite it. It's like what Elizabeth Stuckey-French, author of the critically-loved *Revenge of the Radio Active Lady*, told me in workshop when I was struggling to humanize a villain: "Make him love something you love. You'll have that in common and you'll sympathize with him. Then write from there." Great advice. Thus, my monster got a puppy that afternoon and an affinity for fashion and fine incense.

Some advice from years of my mistakes and fumbling:

1. When possible, give yourself time in the morning. I'm always trying to sleep between 10 PM-6 AM, when you get the best rest. Ease into the day with ritual—you are at your freshest and most open in the morning. Ablutions, yoga, and then journaling over breakfast feel divine and are very productive for me.

2. Eat well and lightly, hydrate, exercise, feel sunshine, and remember to breathe. We all know that our bodies run best on fresh fruits and veggies and plenty of water. Take care of your basics. Don't write all day in the same cramped position and forget to eat (or eat loads of junk). Go outside for your writing breaks instead of going on Facebook. Take meaningful breathers. Minimize pain and discomfort by moving around and listening to your needs. You're human, not a writing machine. Breathe and notice your breath.

3. Make time for your craft, even if it means not answering the phone. Most of the time, you can call friends and loved ones back. Taking time for your art isn't selfish—it's necessary. Read almost as much as you write—read contemporary writing as well as the classics. Read outside the cannon. Read advice from your favorite writers. Make room for yourself. Make room for writing. Make room for rest.

4. Look for joy everywhere. Why not? Chickadees, puppies, full moons, tiny frogs, wild bluebells, beautiful people, skipping, a strange laugh, refreshing gusts of wind, lavender oil…There are a lot of delightful things in the world that conjure feelings. Run with them. Do what makes you happy as often as possible, even if you're writing a sad book. Trust me.

5. Breathe more. Stay present with the breath. Notice.

Remember that making art requires the same focus and intention as spiritual dedication— choose the rituals that suit you and your intentions. You are opening yourself to some force that is not quite explained, whether you like to think of it as the unconscious, the muse, deity, the universe, genius (as in wood spirits), magic, creative energy, or your unfathomable brain. Do so with reverence.

The Frontier of Poetry
Robert Pinsky

A crucial, defining moment happens at the mysterious frontier between mind and body, when a feeling or thought takes form in the voice— possibly as speech, but maybe as less than that, as the exhalation of a barely vocalized *oh* or *ah*.

I mean the moment between the twinge of an aching back muscle and a muttered "ouch" or, at another extreme, the moment when a mix of passion, determination, and purpose leads to "I disagree" in a meeting or "I love you" in an embrace.

We cross that threshold between concept and breath in two directions, I think: outward of course, but inward as well. In an intense conversation, my effort to understand your words —to "take them in," as we say— may include my imagining what it feels like to say those words— physically, actually, to say them. That sympathetic, bodily imagining may go back to the infant gazing up at a parental speaking face: so far back that we are mostly unaware of it.

Sometimes, feeling eager or pressed to understand, I might silently "mouth" your words —technical instructions, say, or the best route to my destination, or just a name or a phone number— form them with my lips, maybe with a whisper of breath through them. (C.K. Williams' great poem "My Mother's Lips" describes this form of attention.)

That basic, intuitive process involves the first principle of reading poetry—the most purely vocal of all the arts. (In song, the voice enlarges and transforms to become an instrument, as well as itself.)

So, the three-word advice I might be tempted to give, about "How to Read a Poem"—*"read it aloud"*—is kind of inaccurate, though usefully compact. "Read it aloud" might lead toward the art of the actor, or the technique of a poet who gives good poetry readings. With all due respect, performance is not what I mean.

I mean something more intimate, more immediate, more physiological, at that mind-body frontier: to feel the poem in your mind's voice, hearing it in your mind's ear as you listen to the things you say. To achieve that kind of attention, you may well say the words—mutter them or declaim them, vocalize them or not— as a means to feel what it would be like to say the poet's words: to *need* to say them, as Emily Dickinson needed to say "Because I could not stop for Death" or Walt Whitman needed to say "Vigil strange I kept in the field one night." If the poem works, the reader experiences an echo of that need. That experience, I think, is demonstrated by the video segments at www.favoritepoem.org.

Here is a specific example of what I mean—one of my favorite examples, because it is brief and to me seems remarkably clear: an untitled, two-line poem by Walter Savage Landor (1775-1864). I invite the reader to say it aloud, or to imagine saying it aloud, maybe moving your lips a little:

On love, on grief, on every human thing,
Time sprinkles Lethe's water with his wing.

The patterns of consonants and vowels in this poem, to me quite beautiful, happen to be unusually clear, by which I mean unusually easy to talk about. At the beginning of the poem, if you say the words, actually or in imagination, three times you will put your upper teeth onto your lower lip to form the "v" or "f" sounds at the ends of "love," "grief," and the first syllable of "every." Another example of this anatomical aspect of poetry, at the end of the poem: three times, you will purse your lips as you say "water with his wing."

Weirdly, but absolutely, such things matter. I cannot explain why, but these patterns of sound (usually not so distinct), apprehended in the body and by the mind, convey feeling. The physical conviction of Landor's poem relieves me of necessarily knowing that Lethe is the river of forgetting in the Classical underground. The poem's physical presence, in my voice, helps me understand that Lethe is what time sprinkles on everything. How do these artfully arranged vowels and consonants, these sentence-sounds, do that? I don't know. I can't explain this vocal-emotional power any more than I can explain the power of music or of comedy (which, the supreme comic Sid Caesar said, *is* music).

Poetry is apprehended by the body and the mind, both. (I think this is why Ezra Pound says, in his *An ABC of Reading*, "poetry is a centaur.") If you are not inclined to use your mind, you will miss the point. If you are not inclined to use your body, in particular breath and the muscles of speech, you will miss the point. True in poetry, and often true in the rest of life, as well.

There has been a lot of excellent writing and thinking about the ways poetry is different from all the other uses of language. It is also worth considering the ways poetry is continuous with the other uses of language, resembles them, from its position somewhere between speech and song.

Poetry is different from but also resembles conversation, teaching, business negotiations, family arguments, joke telling, complaining, medical interviews, and many other kinds of interaction. Facial expression, bodily posture, hand gestures, tone of voice, pace, inflection, all amplify and modify the words—make the words more than a transcript. The equivalent of all that is in a poem, waiting to be animated by each reader's vocal imagination.

How to read a poem? Imagine saying it. Imagine the feeling of needing to say it.

Meditation on Happiness

Ariel Francisco

I want to go through life
with the joy of a bus driver
riding through town in twilight,
catching all the green lights,
smiling softly as he hums along
to the radio and drives right by
all the bus stops, his display
glowing a single gleeful

orange word: *GARAGE.*

Meditation on Patience

Ariel Francisco

Of patience, I know only
what sea turtles have taught me:
how they are born on lightless
beaches so the moon can serve
as a beacon to lure them
into the water; how they spend
their whole lives trying to swim
towards it, enamored, obsessed;
how they flap their forelimbs,
a vague recollection of flying—
the right movement in the wrong
medium, as if they knew how
to reach the moon in a former life
but now only remember the useless
persistent motions; how if you cut
one's heart out it would keep
beating in the pit of your palm,

recognizing the cold night air.

For the Man Pressure Washing the Gas Station Next Door at 1 A.M.

Ariel Francisco

Enough PSI to wake up the whole block,
to rival the airplanes idling across the street,
blast the concrete clean enough to reflect
the neon pink trim of the Airport Diner.
You might as well scrub at the light pollution
to reveal the stars. You're in for a long night.
No one will care. No one will notice.
I suppose you could say the same about
this poem. Don't worry, I wasn't sleeping anyway.

For the Man Pushing His Mixtape on the Corner of Biscayne and 167th

Ariel Francisco

At first I pretend to ignore him,
look forward, nod along to my own
music, but he must have recognized
that hip-hop was what bumped out of
my shit speakers because he persisted,
inspired as he rapped at my window
with his knuckles, saying *c'mon man,*
I know you want this fire like a mischievous
god— and aren't we all entitled to insist
on our art? He especially, fist full
of CD's glinting like otherworldly treasure
in this atrocious summer heat?
I relent, roll down my window, ask
how much? and he's got me, he knows
it, that smirk on his face as the light
turns green and he says *how much you got?*

Symptoms of Prophesy

Camille Rankine

In the new century,
we lose the art of many things.

For example, at the beep, I communicate
using the wrong machine.

I called to say we have two lives
and only one of them is real.

When the phone rings: you could be anybody.
In the evening: you are homeless

and hunting for good light, as safe a place
as any to make a bed for the night.

In both my lives, my nerves go bust.
I'm certain that I'm not

as I appear, that I'm a figment and
you're not really here.

The struggle
is authenticity.

I have a message.
You must believe me.

The Poetry of Protest: A Dozen Pitfalls to Avoid

Marilyn L. Taylor

Virtually everyone who reads poetry nowadays is undoubtedly aware of a vast—and relatively new—sub-category that's become just about unstoppable over the past few decades: *the poetry of protest*. These are poems that won't take no for an answer, refuse to take the world sitting down, never turn the other cheek. It's poetry with an axe to grind, a complaint to register, a bone to pick—and it's been sprouting up everywhere, in every anthology, blog, and journal you can shake a fist at.

Most of us will approach one of these poems of protest knowing very well that it's probably not going to be a mild-mannered meditation on some abstract controversy. On the contrary, the poems' language as well as their tone are likely to be volatile, single-minded, opinionated, emotional, or all of the above. And when it's done well, the effect can be devastating. Think, for instance, of "I, Too" by Langston Hughes, or "The Hand that Signed the Paper" by Dylan Thomas. Or a whole raft of poems by Nikki Giovanni, Marge Piercy, Charles Bukowski, Amiri Baraka, Marilyn Nelson, Philip Levine, June Jordan, many, many others. But far too often, a poem of protest will totally bomb, missing its intended mark entirely.

Why is this the case? Why shouldn't poetry that takes a stand against war, violence, oppression, discrimination, environmental irresponsibility, etc., win universal approval from everybody except the bad guys? My personal theory, which I realize may not be yours, is that the sheer intensity of the poet's commitment to the cause can easily get in the way of the poetry. What started out as a good, strong poem will often morph into a collection of easy slogans and proclamations—frequently accompanied by the deal-breaking assumption that the reader agrees with every word.

Some poems of protest have succeeded remarkably well, of course. Several have actually galvanized thousands into action. A few have even survived their relevant moment in history and become a permanent part of the literary landscape. Henry Reed's wrenching "Naming of Parts," first published in 1946, is one of these, and certainly Allen Ginsberg's "Howl," which in 1956 broke all the rules of propriety, convention, and good manners, and changed the face of poetry in this country forever. An impressive number of other protest poems have succeeded without question (see a few examples listed in the sidebar) —and I'm sure that you yourself could name others right this minute — but many more have evaporated into thin air, no matter how urgent they seemed to be when they were written.

But if you are deeply committed to a particular cause, possibly one that's controversial, and you decide to write a poem about it, I'd like to offer a few tips that could help you avoid the potholes, sandtraps and bottomless pits that could stand in your way:

Avoid over-generalizing. Remember that old adage about *finding the universal in the specific*? It works. Working the other way around (by over-generalizing) can easily lead to making unfair, if not totally false, assumptions. To begin a poem with something like "Kids today! They don't like school. / They drink and smoke and think they're cool" is to make a big mistake. For one thing, the vast majority of kids today don't hate school at all. They're excited and challenged by it, and they think getting an education is what's cool. Second, isn't it likely that the poet is really thinking about one slacker in particular? Maybe a certain distracted one, or a frightened one? Or a bored one, who finished her term paper a month ago and has been playing video games ever since? If your poem focuses on *that particular kid*, it's apt to make its point far more accurately and convincingly.

Do not preach. When you're writing a poem on a subject about which you feel strongly, be very careful about taking a holier-than-thou approach. Sometimes it's difficult to avoid when it seems as though no one out there understands the seriousness of a particular problem quite the way you do. But keep in mind that there are many, many causes out there, and to attract someone to yours means avoiding the accusatory. Here's an example of the sort of thing I'm talking about:

Why can't you see? Why don't you listen?
When will you people finally understand
that (emissions/ discrimination/ deforestation/ sexism) is intolerable?

The assumption here is that the poet sees it, but the rest of us are utterly clueless. It annoys us to be spoken to like that—and the poem won't work.

Avoid telling us what we already know. A poem that spends its time insisting that "Bigotry is wrong!" as if that were some kind of a revelation, is simply not doing its job. Better to point out a specific, unambiguous *example* of bigotry, and give your readers credit for coming to their own conclusions.

Try not to get hysterical. If a poem begins with "Stop it, do you hear? Stop!! Stop!! You are destroying the planet!"—the reader is sorely tempted to say, "Oh shut up" and go about his or her business. An irate, frustrated tone is perfectly okay, but a tantrum rarely succeeds.

Don't settle for easy word-choices. Especially the angry ones, e.g. "Those dirty rotten ******** have ****** us again!" This is not to say that expletives — even the four-letter ones — don't have their place in certain contexts. But the poet who uses them over and over again in the same poem runs two risks: (1) draining all the emphasis and punch from the words in question, and (2) sounding hopelessly juvenile. Let's face it, we've all heard these words before, they no longer shock us, and there are plenty of fresher and more effective alternatives out there.

Do not ignore possible shades of gray: Super-highways are evil? Well, perhaps, in some ways. But what about the congestion they prevent? What about the time-deprived single mother who has to drive to a job in the heart of town? Similarly: If rich people are scorned as arrogant and selfish, what of the enormously generous philanthropists who so often come out of the woodwork to save the day? It's wise to keep in mind that not every issue is a black-and-white issue.

Beware of the second person. It can come across as bossy, even accusatory. Jumping in with "Your candle burns at both ends..." drastically changes both the point and the tone of Edna St. Vincent Millay's famous four-liner, "First Fig." By accusing someone else — possibly the reader — of too much late-night candle-burning, the poem starts sounding cranky, like a disapproving parent.

Do not succumb to stereotyping. "Men are cold-hearted liars" is a line that runs the risk of alienating fifty percent of your readers, namely the men—of whom many are pussycats, and honest, too. A proclamation like this might be fine in certain specialized contexts, of course, if the poet makes it clear that it is either not to be taken literally, or that it is one particular man she has in mind.

Do not sentimentalize: "The poor little homeless puppies / are wagging their tails for love" is pretty saccharine. Of course there's nothing wrong with writing a poem to protest the inhumane treatment of small animals — but attempting to do so with clichés like "poor little," "sweet and innocent," "broken-hearted," or "tear-stained" is a sugar-coated mistake.

Do not get too worked up about the trivial: There are certain small disasters that tend to fill the days of all of us. "My paper towels just don't hold up" is not fodder for true protest. Neither is "dorm food is garbage" or "makeup is way too expensive" or "heavy traffic is a pain."

Do not over-personalize: "I saw my boyfriend with that other girl" might be sad, but it doesn't qualify as a poem of protest because it involves no one except the speaker and her rotten boyfriend. A protest poem worth its salt speaks for many, about something that affects us all.

Avoid preaching to the choir. If you begin a new poem convinced that everyone who reads it will buy what you have to say because you are on the side of the angels, you are making a major mistake. There is likely to be a substantial percentage of your potential readers who hold the opposite view, and it's your job to convince them of the error of their ways. No easy task, but an earnest, well-phrased protest against the status quo will almost certainly help.

Which brings us to an uncomfortable truth that we should remember every time we set out to write a poem that questions the status quo. W. S. Auden probably said it best back in 1939: *Poetry makes nothing happen*. And he's right, of course. But when it's well done, the poetry of protest can do a great deal to show that something very definitely *should* happen. And that, fellow poets, is more than half the battle.

WRITING
EXERCISES

The Writing Exercise: A Recipe

Kathleen Spivack

Ingredients and Preparation:

Before bedtime, pick up the alarm clock. Set it to ring two hours earlier than your usual wake-up time.

Sleep. Or don't. But get up anyway.

Put mug of coffee, tea, or other comfort in your hands. Now go to your desk immediately. Sit down. Look dazed. Open the computer-mind.

Work on a writing project—somehow—for two hours. Don't complain.

Part One.

Do this for two weeks, steadily. Your body may react with fever, aches, and a sense of dullness. Ignore this. It is to be expected.

Part Two.

Do this for two months. Do it for a year. Increase the amount of time spent with your dominatrix. Obey her. Pain, delusions of grandeur, and self-doubt are typical symptoms. Continue. The virus is beginning to take hold.

Part Three.

Congratulations. You are now satisfactorily infected. Write! Do this for the rest of your life.

What's at Stake?

Diana Norma Szokolyai

Any good piece of writing makes clear to the reader what is at stake. But how do we, as authors, clarify what is at stake? First, let us define what we mean by "what is at stake:" It is the central, driving force of a piece. It is what is on the table.

When we talk about what is at stake, we are also talking about investment. It is because a character or speaker is invested that we invest as a reader. Without something at stake, a piece of writing feels flat and is not compelling to read.

In a narrative, if we are to make the experience real for the reader, we must know the why behind everything we write:

-    Why is the character/speaker doing what he/she is doing?
-    Why is the character/speaker thinking what he/she is thinking?
-    What is at stake for the piece of writing overall?

If you don't know why your character or speaker is doing what he or she is doing, then interview him or her. Write a complete backstory. You may not use it all in the narrative, but your research and character mapping will help inform your character's decisions and actions. As real human beings, we do things for a reason, and something is always on the table. For example, when we apply for a new job, we have hopes and insecurities. Make sure your characters have them too. Make sure they are invested in their actions, and then convey that investment through your words.

In Milan Kundera's *The Unbearable Lightness of Being*, Tomas leaves his comfortable job as a surgeon in Vienna in order to be with Tereza, who has returned to her native Prague. He takes a risk by returning, and has his passport confiscated because his relationship with Tereza is at stake. Later, Tomas is informed that he will lose his position as a brain surgeon in Prague unless he signs a declaration taking back his criticism of the Czech communists in a piece he had previously published before the Soviets came to power in 1968. He refuses, loses his position, and is relegated to becoming a window-washer. Tomas's intellectual freedom is at stake, and he sacrifices an illustrious career as a brain surgeon for it. We, as readers, are more moved by his decision to action in both cases because of what is at stake. Because of the political situation in his country, his philosophical stance is at odds with his high social standing. He takes the risk of losing his career, and does, out of personal dignity.

When examining what is at stake, we can also focus on other elements of storytelling. For example, setting is important, as it grounds the reader in a context. It is not effective to take the reader to the ruins of an ancient temple just because it is cool. Choose a setting because it sets up the ideal environment for the action to unfold.

Point of view is very important in a narrative and can also allow for different revelations of investment. The first person can reveal vulnerability very well, or mental instability, secret desires and hopes, unreliability, naïveté, victimization, and narcissism. When we think of a masterful use of the first person, we think of J.D. Salinger's Holden Caulfield in *The Catcher in the Rye*, Nabokov's *Lolita*, Chekhov's *Notes from the Underground*, and Gillian Flynn's *Gone Girl*. Alternating first person narratives have become increasingly popular and offer the power to reveal the secrets of multiple characters' minds. Second person is essential in revealing what is at stake in epistolary novels, text messages, and emails. There are some novels now written entirely in the form of text messages and emails. The third person limited is when the narrator knows only the thoughts and feelings of a single character, and the third person omniscient allows for a lot of flexibility, the ability to zoom in and out. When examining what is at stake, think about how all of these storytelling elements allow for revealing the central driving force of the piece of writing.

Examining what is at stake is not limited to fiction, and is also important in nonfiction and poetry. For any of the exercises below, writers can apply them to examining levels of risk taking for fictional characters, as well as the speakers of poems or the authors themselves.

Exercise One:

If we look at four spheres—the social, the political, the personal, and the professional—we can further examine what is at stake for our characters. This list is not exhaustive, of course, but it can serve as a tool for the writer to explore or expand upon what is at stake for their characters or the speaker of the piece. Also, this list can be used to explore what is at stake in the piece overall. For example, the piece of writing may question a political situation, a social taboo, or a paradigm of thought. Writers may wish to read through the list and highlight what is at stake in their writing, as a self-reflection tool. It can also be used to add new facets of vulnerability to a piece of writing. These lists can also be used in a workshop setting by having writers present pieces of writing in any genre and asking people to identify what is at stake in terms of these four spheres.

Personal:

love, loss, grief, joy, happiness, personal identity, mental stability, personal freedom, agency, free will, sense of control, judgment, relationship to others and to self, sanity, emotional implosions and explosions, fears, biases, religious or spiritual crises, encounters with the unknown, personal gain, greed, lust, jealousy, vices and virtues, reputation, honor, exploitation, betrayal, abuse, intimacy, charisma, transience, vanity, recognition, closure, mortality

Professional:

career, ambition, promotion, reputation, honor, goals, relationships, inferiority and superiority complexes, fear of failure, fear of rejection, overachievement, politics, protection, work vs. personal identity, mentorship, recognition, acknowledgment, vitriol, harassment, glass ceiling, ladder climbing, authority, boy's club, gender and sexual politics, exploitation, betrayal, abuse, culture shock, imbalance, bureaucracy, stereotypes

Social:

belonging, community, social roles, social identity, deviation from group, rebellion, bureaucracy, stereotypes, prejudice, peer group, social expectations, cultural customs, exploitation, betrayal, abuse, online profiling, racial profiling, stereotypes, privacy, exposure, socializing, fraternity, intimacy, understanding, family, liberation, social norms

Political:

stance, beliefs, philosophy, freedom, asylum, persecution, sovereignty, liberation, oppression, reputation, intentions, hierarchy, manipulation, pigeon holing, social responsibility, political identity, affiliation, voice, power, scandal, controversy, hypocrisy, charisma, creating false conflict or resolution

Exercise Two:

Interview your character. Be voyeuristic.

Imagine your character naked.

What is their vulnerability?

What is the last thing they think about before bed?

What do they do or think about after making love?

What do they think about in the shower?

Do they have any strange rituals?

What motivates them?

When you get personal, you can reveal high stakes.

Rasa: Emotion and Suspense in Theatre, Poetry, and (Non)Fiction

Rita Banerjee

Rasa theory centers on taste. Not taste in the sense of sophistication or composure or discernment. Not taste in the sense of good or bad. But taste in its most primal, animalistic, emotive, and provocative form.

Rasa is what happens to you, spectator, reader, part-time lover, when you watch or read a work of art with intensity. Rasa is the flavor of the art experience. It is the feeling produced in the viewer when a work of art is at its most potent and devastating form. Rasa is the immediate, unfettered emotional reaction produced in the spectator when a work of art has left her breathless or yearning for more. Rasa means to savor, to bring a work of art within the body, to let words linger on the tongue. Rasa is a shot to the heart, it's a festering wound, it's the mind at unrest, and it is nobody's captive. It can be dangerous. It can be pleasurable. A visceral form of taste, rasa tends to resist cultivation and containment. Rasa is what happens to you when you find yourself spellbound and alone, and completely enraptured by a work of art for just a moment. It's where the emotional, narrative, and lyrical landscape of a work washes over, prickles, or consumes you. It's the moment where you lose yourself and loosen, and find in your body the first stirrings of emotion.

Rasa is a theory of art that developed in Sanskrit literature at the turn of the common era. Bharata, the great dramaturge, wrote about those unexpected, uncontrollable feelings *(rasas)*, which rise up within the spectator and reader in reaction to the drama and emotions felt between characters on-stage or in-scene. In the *Nāṭyaśāstra (ca. 200 BCE)*, his treatise on the performing arts, storytelling, and effective dramatic and lyrical writing, Bharata outlined eight main emotional states *(sthāyibhāvas)* felt within scene as well as the eight types of emotional responses felt by the viewer *(rasas)*. While Plato argued that human behavior flows from three main sources—desire, emotion, and knowledge—in *The Republic (380 BCE)*, Bharata, in the *Nāṭyaśāstra*, argued that emotion governed all human behavior, psychology, and movement. Harnessing emotion could not only make a poignant and unforgettable work of art, but the writer who engaged and became skilled in this form of aesthetic knowledge could elevate herself to the role of an artist. Rasa theory is thus a treatise on how to effectively represent emotions and create suspense, forward momentum, and surprise in a work of art. Successful use of rasa engages a viewer in an artwork. The viewer who experiences an artwork does not necessarily undergo a moment of catharsis in rasa theory, but rather produces an individual, spontaneous, emotional, psychological, and bodily feeling towards that work of art.

In fact, one of the topics that is often hotly debated in rasa theory centers on the idea of catharsis and tragedy. In classical Greek dramaturgy, the theatrical mode of tragedy focuses on the feelings of fear and pity produced within the spectator. In the Aristotelian mode, a spectator becomes so enraptured with the drama on stage that she cannot separate herself from the actions, psychology, and emotions of the characters in-scene, and thus, the spectator becomes the character in a sense. Only when the play ends is the spectator released from the drama she has witnessed and consumed. This moment of release, of purging the emotions of fear and pity after witnessing a tragedy, is often interpreted as catharsis. In Bharata's model, however, when a spectator witnesses a moment of grief, distress, or suffering on stage or in-scene, she does not necessary feel the same tragic elements or pain herself, but rather responds with compassion or empathy.[6] That is, rasa theory argues that the spectator comes to the theatre with a cool eye and a bit of ice in her heart. The spectator is always actively interpreting what is happening in-scene and on-stage. She assumes an emotional, intellectual, and critical distance from a work of art. In order to be effective, a work of art must bridge the emotional, intellectual, and critical divide between the spectator and the actors on stage. In rasa theory, a work of art only has power if it is able to elicit a response in the spectator, preferably an emotional or bodily one.

In the 10th Century CE, another Sanskritic aesthetician, Abhinavagupta, partly inspired by the egalitarian Bhakti devotional movement which demolished religious, class, and gender stigmas and taboos, argued that hu-

---

6 Thus, many provocateurs have raised the question: can tragedy exist within Sanskrit theatre and literature?

mans could enter a state where strong emotions were laid to rest, a state in which a sense of serenity, calm, and satisfaction prevailed. He thus argued to add a ninth rasa of *śānta (peace)* to Bharata's original eight categories.

Following the tradition of rasa, Kālidāsa (ca. 4th-5th Century CE) would become famous for employing rasa theory effectively in his writing, and seducing the viewer with emotion in his most famous works of theatre and poetry. In Kālidāsa's *The Recognition of Śakuntalā (ca. 4th Century CE)*, much like the opening of Goethe's *Faust, Part 1 (1808)*, the narrative begins with a metatextual moment, a play within a play when the director and actress talk about what kind of emotional performance and storytelling would most effectively capture the heart of the audience.

In the prologue, the director challenges his actress-lover: "As though in a painting, the entire audience has had their emotion colored through your melody. So now—what shall we perform to sustain the mood?" In this exercise, we will explore how creating vivid emotional worlds between characters and within storylines can build suspense, sustain drama, and lure the reader deeper in.

First, let's take a look at the nine main categories of the latent emotions *(sthāyibhāvas)* experienced by actors and characters within a scene and the emotional moods, feelings, or emotional interpretations created within the audience *(rasas)* as described by Bharata and Abhinavagupta: [7]

Sthāyibhāvas – latent or dominant emotions felt by actors, characters, or speakers in-scene

Rati – *sexual love, desire, lust*
Hāsa – *laughter, merriment, hijinks*
Śoka – *grief, distress, suffering*
Krodha – *anger, rage*
Utsāha – *masterfulness, courage, triumph*
Bhaya – *fear, terror*
Jugupsā – *disgust, revulsion*
Vismaya – *wonder, astonishment*
Śama – *quietude, coming to a state of rest*

---

[7] Translations of these categories are inspired by Dharwadkhar (1400) and Rao (59).

Rasas – feelings, *emotive moods, emotional interpretations, or emotional reactions experienced by the reader or the audience*

Śṛṅgāra – *love, romance*
Hāsya – *the comic, amusement, mirth, joy*
Karuṇā – *pathos, compassion*
Raudra – *anger, fury*
Vīra – *the heroic*
Bhayānaka – *fear*
Bībhatsa – *disgust, repulsion*
Adbhuta – *wonder, surprise*
Śānta – *tranquility, calm, satisfaction, peace*

The emotions (*bhāvas*) felt in-scene produce an echo, reverberation, effect or suggestion (*dhvani*) on the audience. The four major forms of acting (*abhinaya*) which draw out and convey an emotion from a work of art to the spectator include gesture (*āṅgika abhinaya*), speech (*vācika abhinaya*), setting and costuming (*āhārya abhinaya*), and a character's internal psychology (*sāttvika abhinaya*).

The fun part about rasa theory is that since Bharata's first call to arms to writers and artists in the *Nāṭyaśāstra (ca. 200 BCE)*, the idea of categorizing and numbering emotions has been in debate for centuries. From the 9th to 11th centuries CE, Abhinavagupta and Ānandavardhana tried to embellish upon and expand Bharata's eight classical categories for *rasa* and definitions of *dhvani (suggestion)*, respectively. And in the 20th century, literary critic and theorist Dipti Tripathi noted something interesting going on with rasa theory in the modernist literature coming out of Bengal. She argued to redefine the traditional rasa categories of *adhbhuta* as "not wonder, but a sense of the uncanny, the abnormal, the strange, estrangement, and absurdity," and *bībhatsa* as "not just disgust, but a focus on monstrosity and the grotesque, and a sense of repulsion related to monstrosity." Tripathi also emphasized auxiliary emotions as major rasas as in the case of *vyaṅga*, which indicated "mockery, irony, sarcasm, dark humor, or schadenfreude," and *vitaraka*, which indicated "debate, controversy, argument, deliberation, and doubt" (Banerjee xii, 42). These emotions and feelings, Tripathi argued, represented the new emotional landscape of the modern individual affected by war, famine, partition and mass-migration, industry, urbanization, isolation, existentialism, and the rise of psychoanalysis.

So how can we use rasa to create artwork that responds with vivid precision to the realities of the 21st century? Let's roll up our sleeves, writer, and see if we can have a little fun using the elements of rasa theory to create vivid emotional landscapes, suspense, and forward momentum in our own works of art.

Prompt 1:

On nine flashcards, write down the nine key in-scene *bhāvas*, or emotions (i.e. sexual love/desire, laughter/merriment, grief/distress, anger/rage, courage/ triumph, fear/terror, disgust/revulsion, wonder, and quietude). On four additional flashcards, write down the four forms of *abhinaya* or acting (i.e. gesture, speech, mise-en-scène, and internal psychology). Now pick a card from each pile. See if you can convey the emotion listed on the card through the form of acting suggested. Compose a scene, a poem, a story, a flashback, an essay, etc. in which the dominant emotion of the piece is the one listed on your *bhāva*-card. See if you can make that emotion echo and manifest through the form of acting suggested. Have a friend read through your work or read it out loud to an audience. What does your audience feel when they hear your work? What kind of emotional reactions *(rasas)* are evoked in them?

Prompt 2:

In this exercise, let's expand upon and play with the traditional categories of rasa theory. Make the nine classical rasa cards and make four cards listing the "modernist" rasas (i.e. dark humor/irony/mockery, argument/doubt, the uncanny/absurdity/estrangement, and a reaction to the grotesque/monstrous). To this mix, add any additional emotions or mix of feelings you think are missing.[8] In this prompt you will be working with two different characters within a scene. Pick one rasa card for each character. Set these two characters up in a scene where they have to interact. But when these characters encounter one another, make sure they can barely contain their

---

[8] For a complete list of auxiliary emotions (vyabhichārī bhāvas), see Dharwadkher 1398, 1400.

individual emotional states within the scene. What happens when these two characters meet? Does the tension between them dry up or fester or sugar over or sag like a heavy load, or does it explode?

Prompt 3:

If you're working on a longer narrative or a book-length manuscript, you may want to map out the text in terms of emotion. Does your manuscript have a little love, a little laughter, a little sadness, a little anger, a little triumph, a little fear, a little disgust, a little surprise, and a little satisfaction in it? If you find that many successive scenes or segments of your book-length work are bottled up with the same emotion, you might want to cut-and-paste these sections elsewhere to create some tension and suspense in your book. Think of your book-length manuscript as a project showcasing a continual or gradual transformation of emotion. Hook in your reader by keeping the emotional landscape of your work varied and alive. As the Comedian suggests in the opening prelude of Goethe's *Faust*, suspense can be created through the anticipation or the lack of release of emotion.

<u>Suggested Readings:</u>

Banerjee, Rita. *The New Voyager: Theory and Practice of South Asian Literary Modernisms*. Harvard University, Dissertation. Cambridge, MA: ProQuest, 2013.

Choudhary, Satya Dev. *Glimpses of Indian Poetics: A Survey of Sanskrit Poetics*. New Delhi: Sahitya Akademi, 2002.

Dharwadker, Vinay. "Emotion in Motion: The *Nāṭyashāstra*, Darwin, and Affect Theory." *PMLA, Volume 130, Number 5*. New York: Modern Language Association, October 2015.

Rao, Valli. "Suggestive Taste of Theory: *Rasa* and *Dhvani* in Hiriyanna's *Art Experience*." *Indian Literary Criticism in English: Critics, Texts, Issues*. Ed. P.K. Rajan. Jaipur: Rawat Publications, 2004.

Sheldon, Pollock. *A Rasa Reader: Classical Indian Aesthetics*. New York: Columbia University Press, April 2016.

---. "From Rasa Seen to Rasa Heard." *Aux abords de la clairière*. Ed. Caterina Guenzi and Sylvia d'Intino. Paris: Brepols, Collections érudites de l'École Pratique des Hautes Études, 2012.

Quiet Mayhem in Fiction: A Writing Exercise

Forrest Anderson

Each semester, I open my undergraduate fiction workshop by distributing and reading from the first 'real' short story I ever wrote as a twenty two year old. It is as bad as a first story can be (and much worse if I'm being honest)—a town floods during a record-setting hurricane, a power plant explodes killing dozens of innocent people in lush detail, a man caught without a life vest in a swollen river gets struck dead by a bass boat piloted by quarreling rednecks, and an old woman left strapped to her bed in an evacuated nursing home drowns while she remembers swim lessons with her father… I killed her dog, too, to heighten the emotional tension.

Plenty's wrong with the story—more teachable moments than I can bring myself to admit—but what I choose to focus on is a lesson that I was slow to learn: a writer doesn't need to flood a story with twists and turns and improbable events to hold a reader's attention. Instead, a writer should approach 'high events' or moments of dramatic intensity with an accompanying subtlety to maintain the tone and integrity of literary fiction. Put simply, a reader's curiosity should be about *what happens next* in the story, not what will the writer *dream up next*.

I didn't understand the importance of subtlety until I read Douglas Bauer's *The Stuff of Fiction: Advice on Craft*. Bauer draws a distinction between readers of commercial fiction and readers of literary fiction. Like commercial readers, literary readers ask themselves, "What happens?" but what they respond to is "the continuing call of *one* thing, or a few things, rather than to the easily and carelessly digested sequence of many things" (Bauer 127). Effective storytelling, according to Bauer, varies its pace, "as the writer swiftly summarizes the story and alternately pauses to make a scene, for which he must slow down in order to inspect closely and report the details" (128). 'High events' are a powerful way to slow down narrative and create an image or scene that resonates throughout a story. Writers who can effectively render subtle high events can get away with murder, kidnapping, lust, romance, and "all manner of mayhem and marvel and emotional extreme" (125).

Bauer offers three ways that subtlety can be applied to high event:

1. Describe violence in a counterintuitive tone, whether it be one of romance or myth or comic action or some other.

2. Direct the narrative circuitously, seemingly even casually, toward the high event, garnering a kind of momentum of obliqueness by insisting readers first attend to the details or the consequences before they encounter the moment that produced them.

3. Strategically place the high event itself at the very edge of the narrative's frame of vision, maybe even entirely outside of it. (129)

To turn subtlety into a writing exercise, I provide the below handout which pairs Bauer's strategies with several examples of high events grouped by dead bodies, children, love, and violence. I ask students to pick one strategy and one high event and write the scene. Often, students will experiment with all three strategies and multiple events. Some of the events described come from published stories and novels (others come from that wild place inside me that dreamed up my first 'real' story). I've noted the published works in case you want to use them as models of high event and accompanying subtlety in classroom discussion.

THE STRATEGY (FROM DOUGLAS BAUER)

• Violence in a counterintuitive tone
   o   Elevate it to a tone of romance
   o   Make it highly romantic
   o   Make it comic
• Arrive at the violence circuitously
   o   Insist that the reader attend to the details or the consequences before encountering the moment which produced them
• Place the high event at the edge of the narrative's frame of vision, even outside of it

THE HIGH EVENT

- Dead Body
  - o   Your character(s) go trout fishing and find a dead body floating face down in the river (adapted from "So Much Water So Close to Home" by Raymond Carver)
  - o   Your character witnesses a school bus crash and he or she isn't sure if the number of the bus is his or her own child's (adapted from *The Sweet Hereafter* by Russell Banks and "Valor" by Richard Bausch)
  - o   Your character takes out the trash and finds a dead body stuffed in his yard cart
- Children
  - o   A child steps out to cross the street and gets creamed by an ice-cream truck (adapted from "The Bath" and "A Small, Good Thing" by Raymond Carver)
  - o   Two children fistfight in the backyard (adapted from "Refresh, Refresh" by Benjamin Percy)
  - o   A kid buries a cat to its neck in the dirt and then runs it over with a lawn mower
  - o   A teenager shoots the two-story inflatable Santa Claus in front of a Christmas tree lot
  - o   Your character sees a woman beat the hell out of her child in Wal-Mart
- Love
  - o   Your character walks in to his or her home and finds his or her significant other "holding hands" with his or her best friend (adapted from *Sula* by Toni Morrison)
  - o   Your character's twenty-four-year-old daughter tells him that she's marrying a sixty-three-year-old man (adapted from "Aren't You Happy for Me?" and "Not Quite Final" by Richard Bausch)
  - o   Your character's father calls him or her to a hotel and asks him or her to take his lover out of town (very loosely adapted from "Death of a Salesman" by Arthur Miller and "Great Falls" by Richard Ford)

- Violence
  - o   Two women fistfight in the street (adapted from "Pornography" by Steve Almond)
  - o   A man loses his arm to a piece of industrial machinery
  - o   A man is run over by a train
  - o   A deer hunter draws a bead on another hunter

The Craft of Travel Writing
Shawn Wong

Facts, statistics, dates are quickly forgotten; images are not soon forgotten. Your job on this trip is to collect and record images as well as experiences.

Assignment #1: Buy a Journal

Tell a simple story about where, how and why you chose the journal you bought.

Your journal is your workbook. Use it to record the things that your camera can't capture.

- Overheard conversations while riding on the bus.
- What does a city sound like at different times of the day?
- What does it feel like to stand next to a famous landmark for the first time? What happened there in history? Did an empire end here? Who else stood here?
- What is the relationship in physical size between you and a landmark such as the Reichstag building in Berlin? What does it feel like to be at an ancient gate to a walled city?
- Draw something in your journal instead of taking a picture.
- Write down recipes, gossip, foreign words, graffiti, even useless phrases that you know you will never use.
- Glue things into your journal.
- Have other people write in your journal. For example, if you hear an interesting phrase, ask the person to write it down in your journal.
- Draw a map with your own personal landmarks. Keep adding things to the map as you discover new things.
- Visit the same site two or three times and record how each visit is different.
- Leave your camera in your room on some days and just bring your journal.

How To Write In Your Journal

Instead of making your entries oriented solely to what you did that particular day, try thinking of a particular image from that day and focus your writing on that image and work your writing around it. Work your writing backwards from that image to how you got there, what you did prior to that, etc. What images did you notice on your first day in a new city? What did you focus on when you knew your neighborhood better? What images did you see every day? In other words, drive your story with an image, an object, an interesting character, even a phrase.

- Try to avoid writing in the passive voice. It weakens and dulls your prose, particularly if you use too many passive sentences. For example: "Istanbul was visited by our class and a great lunch was consumed at the Istanbul Culinary Institute by all." Passive. The subject of the sentence should do the acting rather than being acted upon. Active.

- Try not to use too many adverbs in your descriptions. "The view was amazingly and stunningly beautiful." That tells the reader nothing; be more specific.

- Proofread, proofread, proofread. Proofread your work before turning it in. Check spelling, especially place names. Don't guess. Be precise, be accurate, care about the work you turn in.

- Try to make a simple sentence a more complex one. Dress up a sentence with dependent or independent clauses. If you dare, use a semicolon or something outrageous like that. Write a sentence with eight words, then one with twelve words, then eight, then some other pattern. Or, try not using any words that have the letter "a" in it—it forces you to see something else in your writing, to discover a trick in the language by accident. In other words, make yourself write differently. Do something ungrammatical for effect, like a one-word sentence. Take a risk.

- When you are writing your assignments, think about how your writing "sounds." Lots of you play a musical instrument and you know that you can play the notes correctly, but you're not really communicating the feeling and emotional texture of the piece you're playing. Writing is the same thing. After you finish an assignment, "listen" to the word choices you've made. Push yourselves to move your writing ability to another level. You are surrounded daily by languages other than English. Try to make your writing different in Berlin and Istanbul and Rome and Beijing than it is at home. Move your pen in new directions.

- Read the drafts of your writing and ask yourself if what you wrote could be written at home just as well. If you read over a draft of a writing assignment and it bores you, then it will bore other readers as well.

- Tell a story, rather than listing experiences in chronological order. I once took three students to a pasta museum in Rome. I told the woman that I needed one adult ticket (10 Euro) for me and three student tickets (1 Euro each). She told me that I needed to buy three adult tickets and one student ticket, explaining that the one female student with me could pay 1 Euro, but the two males had to pay the full adult rate. I asked why and all she said, in English, was that the boys were "too big." I told her, in Italian, that they were the same age as the girl (who was very petite). She just repeated, "Too big." I paid the inflated rate and told the boys they had to stoop down next time I bought tickets or wait around the corner. That experience says so much about Rome. Sometimes I go to a museum and just tell them that I have a group of students and I'd like to get in free. It actually works about 50% of the time. Or, I say that I'm the teacher so I shouldn't have to pay. It's called "acting Italian."

- Use your roommate and other students as your peer reviewers. Read the blog and see what other students in prior classes have written. You can even quote from each other's writing.

What To Write In Your Journal

You have a journal. You have blank pages in it. Scary proposition, man. What to do? Your journal is your workbook for drafts, observations, incomplete thoughts, etc. and the writing in your blog is where you put your final, polished versions of your writing you want others to read. Journal is inward looking and your blog is outward looking.

I encourage you to plan your own field trips in your spare time or figure out where organized field trips end and what you can see near there. You can explore on your own or in a small group. Go back and look at something by yourself that you visited in a group. Write about getting yourself to a site as well as writing about the site itself. Show somebody something you've discovered on your own. Write about something you haven't seen or experienced and then write about it after you've visited that site. What you write about doesn't even have to be important. For example, what do you see on TV that's different from American TV? Tell a story about buying something.

When you were a child, you learned new words every day. Be a child again. Learn five new foreign words a day.

Write sensory images. One evening in Florence, Italy I ate "filetto di aceto balsamico"—a steak fillet drowned in a balsamic vinegar reduction so thick it made the steak black. It was so delicious, I didn't want to eat anything the next day for fear that I would lose the taste bud memory on my tongue. Write that.

Make your writing have that quality about it that required you to *be* in that city or country. What does it feel like to be in a city where the ghost of that history is embedded in the soul of the city?

Think about the contrasts of old and new, sound and silence, light and dark. Is the quality of the light different where you are and where you come from? Does it smell differently?

Assignment #2: The Ubiquitous Postcard

This assignment is very, very simple. When you're out and about on the streets of a city either on a class field trip or on your own, buy a postcard of something that you're actually looking at or standing in front of. Try to position yourself in the same place as the photographer of the postcard. On the back of the postcard, write down the things that aren't in the picture—sounds, smells, things outside the border of the picture you're holding—anything that strikes you as interesting to note. What this exercise does is capture a precise experience at a precise moment. Call it "writing of the moment." Number the postcard or date it so that you know the order of the postcards. *Do this postcard assignment every day.* At the end of the class you will have a postcard of every day. Place them in order and you have an interesting diary. Do not buy a postcard and then write on the back later when you're not standing in position—that defeats the purpose.

Assignment #3: Writing a City

Berlin's story is all about the 20th century and *Istanbul's* story is all about antiquity. In Istanbul, the writer Orhan Pamuk writes about the melancholy of Istanbul, the ruin of an empire and W.G. Sebald, in *The Emigrants*, writes about the haunting presence and memory of Germany's tragic place in the 20th century. Both books are clearly about memory and both use visual images to help tell the story, provoke a memory, freeze time.

Describe being in one foreign city and what you brought with you as you traveled to another foreign city. Did some part of living in one city create a cultural lens through which you viewed the next city? What does it feel like to have these other "borders" between you and home?

Read an author's account of growing up in a foreign city and try to write like him or her. Write about memory, reality, and even hallucination. Pamuk writes about seeing Istanbul in black and white. In the 14th century people trusted their memories more than reality. To them, wearing eyeglasses actually distorted their view of the world—they trusted the memory of something more than the thing itself. A frescoed wall was meant to inform you what the world or afterlife was really like. People lived inside walled cities. Owning books was for rich people. Writing was art. Making paper and ink and writing was a labor-intensive craft. And after you wrote something, it had to be protected. Both Sebald and Pamuk write as if they're protecting memory.

Flaubert wrote, "The melancholy of the antique world seems to me more profound than that of the moderns, all of whom more or less imply that beyond the dark void lies immortality. But for the ancients that 'black hole' is infinity itself; their dreams loom and vanish against a background of immutable ebony. No crying out, no convulsions—nothing but the fixity of the pensive gaze." He was writing about Rome, but his statement applies so perfectly to other situations. What are the places or sites that make Flaubert's statement ring true?

When you come back to a city you've visited before, does it feel like you're coming "home?" Why? Is there an exact moment in your time in that city where you feel that you *belong* there and the summer tourists taking pictures of everything and carrying fanny packs look horribly out of place?

Assignment #4: Memory

After you've finished the postcard assignment and traveled back home, assemble all the postcards in chronological order. Now write something from memory that occurred between each postcard. Make that entry something sensory—a new taste on your tongue, a sound you heard only at night when other sounds faded away, the smell of rain, food, the subway, the feel of an ancient stone wall, perhaps even a dream about being at home with your family. At the end of this writing project, you will have both writing of the moment on site and writing from memory.

Writers on Location: Nature Writing Prompt

Suzanne Van Dam

Note to Teacher: Nature writing can be a real snooze, like the Christmas card addressed to everyone in general and interesting to no one in particular. Natural images are more effective when grounded in dramatic conflict. They need urgency and purpose, or all those landscape descriptions become self-indulgent trips down memory lane. But nature writing can be powerful too, for a strong sense of place adds authenticity and poignancy.

This exercise introduces a sense of pathos and longing into the natural setting and requires students to consider their audience. The tension of the piece heightens as the students ground their descriptions of nature in a shared emotional experience that they have with someone whom they love but may never see again. This exercise can help students find a story within their brief encounter with nature, nudging them to select meaningful, vivid details that will evoke some emotional response. The field notes provide the specificity to ground the piece in both body and place.

This writing prompt works well in a class or workshop but requires some time in between, such as a break of several hours or an evening in order to complete both parts. I usually allow 35-45 minutes for Part I and give them only Part I directions at first, withholding Part II until after they return from the woods with their field notes. It is better for them to freely take note of what they see/experience and later use those physical details as a springboard for the second part rather than prematurely censoring what they observe.

Directions to Students/Writers:

Part I: Go off by yourself and journal about your surroundings here in the woods, writing down whatever comes to you—what you see, feel, hear, taste, smell, etc. Pay special attention to your body— how your body experiences this environment. But don't just take it in, TAKE NOTES, pages of them, as detailed as possible. You will be surprised by how much you forget later on.

Part II: To be done at home. Take out your field notes and reread them. Then, think of someone about whom you care deeply but who is no longer available to you. By that, I mean someone who you can no longer talk to because he/she is absent from your life—a grandparent who has passed away, an estranged friend, a brother or sister overseas in the military, etc. Hold that person in your mind. Next, re-imagine being out in the woods and then draft a letter to this person, describing your experience—what you thought, felt, saw, heard. Use your physical surroundings in nature as a touchstone to recall a shared memory or to tell that person something important you wish you'd said earlier. Think of this as your last shot, your last chance at sharing where you are and what you need to say.

Using Visuals to Develop
Inner and Outer Stories
Rachael Hanel

Is there an image that haunts you? Is there an object that you're reluctant to part with? Mine these visuals for their deeper meanings, and you will have a winning formula for an essay or collection of essays.

My memoir started with one image that I couldn't shake. My dad worked as a gravedigger in a small Minnesota town, and when I was little, I would go with him to the cemeteries. In one of our cemeteries, there was a small gravestone with a photograph on it. This was the late 1970s, and it was unusual to find a photograph on a gravestone. I was young, barely able to read, so the picture spoke to me in ways that words yet could not.

The photo was of a fifteen-year-old girl. I thought she was beautiful, with her apple cheeks, red hair, and white, even teeth. She wore a green shirt; the wide collar was visible at the bottom of the frame. Vicki died in 1976. I couldn't believe someone like her could be dead. In the picture, she looked so healthy and full of life. She should have been in school, hatching weekend plans with her friends in the hallways. She should have been at home, daydreaming about her future, wondering what she would do, where she would live. For years, every time I went to the cemetery, I would visit Vicki's grave. In a way, I grew up with her; she was like an older sister.

By the time I got to college, my dad had been dead a few years and I hadn't been to cemeteries since. But the image of Vicki would come back to me time and again.

In college, I enrolled in a creative nonfiction class, and that's where I first wrote about Vicki. I described the gravestone and her photograph, but now I also thought more about what the picture meant to me. Why did I continue to think about it all these years later? While writing the essay, I discovered that Vicki was more than just a haunting photograph. As I wrote, the words on the page showed that she had provided a major revelation to my younger self: Vicki was my first introduction to the idea that young people could die. Most children are shielded from the facts of mortality, but by virtue of my dad's job, I was not. Suddenly, I had an essay in which I could ponder "big" questions. How did the knowledge of early mortality affect me? How did it shape my life?

After writing the essay, I felt that I had only started to answer those questions. So I continued to explore my childhood through additional images culled from my time in cemeteries. I wrote about going to the wake of a young mother and her daughter who died in a house fire just a few months after the mother had remarried. The mother was laid out in her wedding gown, and the daughter wore her white flower girl dress. They looked like princesses. I wrote about the shock of seeing a 24-foot-long gravestone, under which are buried a mother and her six children, victims of a car-train accident in 1959. I wrote about another photo on a gravestone of a county sheriff killed in the line of duty. I wrote about trinkets and flowers left on baby graves and about small country churches and graveyards that dotted the countryside. When I was fifteen years old, the image became much more personal. I wrote about seeing my dad in his casket. Now, the inner story took on a new meaning. While I had grown up around death, I discovered that I had no knowledge of grief. I was raised in the Midwest, surrounded by people who kept their emotions quietly tucked away. After Dad died, I was forced to navigate this new world of grief primarily on my own.

When I first wrote about Vicki, I had no idea it would lead to an entire book. I developed the following exercise based on how I wrote that first essay. The exercise helps to develop the important inner story—the part of the story that uncovers a universal theme readers can relate to. I could write a lovely description of Vicki's picture, which would be the outer story. But description alone would not provide the connection that readers need. However, if I also write about grief, loss, and mortality, suddenly my essay has themes that everyone can relate to. Vicki's picture simply provides the specific detail needed to deliver themes to readers in a way they can understand.

The writer Vivian Gornick calls this "the situation and the story." In her book on personal narrative of the same title, she writes: "The situation is the context or circumstance, sometimes the plot; the story is the emotional experience that preoccupies the writer: the insight, the wisdom, the thing one has come to say." Without both, an effective personal essay cannot exist.

I've used this exercise to great effect in workshops. I often ask participants to share their writings, and they tell me amazing personal stories. Every story generated from these workshops would be worthy of at least an essay, if not an entire manuscript. No matter its length, a story must begin somewhere. In this exercise, it begins with one image.

Exercise:

Is there an image that keeps haunting you? Something that you cannot forget even years later? A photograph, or a memory burned brightly on your mind, or the color of your mother's dress at that one holiday party? This image is sticking with you for a reason. Honor it by writing about it.

You also can do this exercise with an object. Is there an object that you continue to hang on to? A teddy bear, a porcelain figurine, a poster? Something that you take with you as you move from place to place? Maybe it looks out of place amid your other possessions. Do other people ask you why you keep it?

Take a few minutes and write a description of the image or object. Imagine that you're a reporter; simply describe it as you would to another person. What is its shape? Color? What details can you focus on? This is the outer story.

Now, on a separate piece of paper, try to attach a meaning to the image or object. In the case of an image, why do you continue to think about it? For an object, why do you still have it? What does it represent? What is the larger story that can be told about the image or object? Identify a universal theme for that larger story. Universal themes are ideas that most everyone can relate to, i.e. loss, love, work, relationships, etc. This will be the inner story.

Now that you've identified both the outer story and inner story, you can start to write a well-rounded essay. Blend the two together, trying to achieve a balance between inner and outer story. If you're like me, you might ask yourself, "Is there more where this came from?" If so, you might find yourself writing several essays revolving around one universal theme that could eventually be linked together into a manuscript.

Attributes: A Prompt
Kevin McLellan

1. Identify a person who influenced you as a child. Set a timer for at least three minutes, close your eyes, and meditate on this person, taking careful mental note of each resonant detail.

2. Once your meditation is complete, make a list (i.e., words, phrases, lines) of these details, say, nine.

3. Add three concrete nouns and three uncommon verbs that distinctly represent you to this list.

4. Write a poem to this influential person or a self-portrait poem. Try to incorporate as many of these words, phrases, and lines from your list into your poem, yet also include other necessary details that are not a part of your list.

5. Once you have written through the poem, place this draft in an envelope and seal it. Place the envelope with your poem in a cupboard or under your bed or in the attic, someplace out of sight.

6. Take a deep breath or a nap.

7. Retrieve the envelope with your poem approximately one week later. Before you open it, meditate once more on this same person and record any additional details.

8. Now open the envelope and read your first draft aloud. Are there any extraneous words? If so, cut them. Are there any gaps? If so, do any of these new details have a place here? If not, create a phrase or line to act as a bridge between each gap.

9. Read your poem aloud once more. Is the form best supporting the emotionality and/or intelligence of the poem? Or is a form being forced upon the poem? Continue to revise as necessary.

10. Take a deep breath or a nap.

11. If your poem needs more attention, repeat steps 5 through

12. Please note: revision is vital, quotidian, a process not dissimilar to breathing.

Summer-Inspired Writing Prompts
Anca L.Szilágyi

We're deep into summer. So, how are you going to get any dang writing done when everything is so easy-breezy? That's how it feels in Seattle, at least, when, after ten months of rain, we blink up at the sun, smile dumbly, and forget what we were doing. Who wants to hunch over a computer when it's gorgeous outside?

Or maybe you're not dizzy from sun poisoning. Maybe you're coming back from a writing conference, still processing the stack of feedback you received on your work-in-progress. Maybe you want to start something new before tackling that revision. (I highly recommend starting something new before tackling that revision.)

Either way, instead of writing a long introduction on the merits of summer (I mean, really), I went gonzo on the prompts. So grab a lightweight notebook, find yourself a shady perch, and get writing. There's at least 300 minutes of hot, hot writing here.

Five-minute prompts
1. List all the scary things you associate with summer. (For example, I always hated watching amateur fireworks from my grandmother's roof in Brooklyn for fear of said fireworks landing on said roof.)
2. List all the things you associate with fireworks.
3. List all the beautiful things you associate with summer.
4. List all of your dream summer vacations.
5. List all the people in your life you associate with summer.
6. List all the *textures* you associate with summer. (Yes, you could do each of the other senses too.)
7. In as much detail as possible, describe the physical sensation of sunburn.

Ten-minute prompts

1. Write a scene using the words lobster, melon, and urine.
2. Describe the worst summer you ever had. Describe the best.
3. Write a scene involving a boat.
4. Write a scene about heat. Write about the hottest place you've ever been.
5. Describe the weirdest summer camp you can imagine.
6. Write a scene involving chlorine.
7. Write a scene using the words snorkel, flummox, kale, and dendochronology.
8. What is your earliest memory of summer?

Twenty + minute prompts

1. Write about a dream vacation that goes wrong in exactly the worst possible way. (Once I took a class with Heather McHugh, and she told us, "When you're stuck, think of whatever would be most unholy. Then write that." This advice seems appropriate here.)
2. Write a story around the ideas of ripening and rotting.
3. Rewrite *Jaws* from the perspective of the shark.
4. Write a story within a time frame of one day. (Hint: July 20 is apparently Ugly Truck Day.)
5. Write a story using the words blithesome, baseball, fruit salad, and schadenfreude.
6. List all the books you associate with summer. Use the words from their titles to write a story.
7. Do you like to write stories based on historical research? In Edvard Munch's time, it was fashionable to sunbathe in the nude. Write a story about the time Munch went to the beach at Warnemunde to recover from a complicated relationship and to "bring back his vitality."

Ray Bradbury's *The Illustrated Man* was my summer reading assignment going into the eighth grade. In addition to the regular, run-of-the-mill essay in response, we got to write a story in the style of Bradbury, and I wrote about an expedition to the center of the sun. That's how much I used to hate summers in New York; I felt as if I were boiling inside the sun. By contrast, summers in Seattle are tepid and cool. No matter what kind of summer you're having, I hope you're writing copiously.

Listening to Winter
S.D. Lishan

To listen means to be quiet oneself. It is an action demanding inaction, requiring reception.
—Jane Hirschfield

As I write this sentence in early December, heavy snow storms are rummaging through the heartland and are moving east. According to the Weather Channel, travel plans will be thrown into a tizzy for much of the country as snow and icy rain delay plane and car travel. Where I live, in Ohio, between two to four inches of snow is predicted tonight, along with rain and sleet. Temperatures are expected to fall into the teens. Ah, I think, perfect! What a great time to ponder poetry-writing and winter!

The following is an assignment that I've constructed for my students at the Ohio State University. It will take you out of your comfort zone, literally, and make you go outside into the winter, to hang out alone, to listen, and to write. The assignment is called "'For the Listener, who listens…' Listening to Winter."

The title of this writing assignment comes from that famous poem by Wallace Stevens, "The Snow Man," and in my class the preparation for the assignment involves students gathering around in a group outside, bundled up against cold, and listening to Stevens's poem. We also share out loud poems about winter by Robert Frost and Tomas Transtromer, as well as a lovely excerpt from a little prose piece by Jane Hirschfield about listening, in which she focuses on that famous passage in *Song of Myself,* section 26, as Walt Whitman declares that he will do "nothing but listen." We read that bit of Whitman, too, as well as a wonderful poem by Mark Svenvold called "Ceiba Tree, Petac, Mexico" about listening to the racket of sound coming from a ceiba tree in a forest in the Yucatan. I encourage you to do the same, albeit with different poems perhaps, and perhaps in a warmer place than outside, but please, to prepare yourself, read some poems out loud, listen; feel the words tumble through your body.

Then, if you aren't there already, go outside, into the cold, into winter. In my classes, we spread out among the acreage on our campus's restored prairie. It gives us plenty of space to be alone, to listen, and then to write. Where you are will be different of course, but, please, go, get outta the "here" where you are now, all cozy and comfy. Go outside into a different "now." Find your own special place to be alone, to listen, and then to write.

I'll show you the assignment in a moment, but first here is a poem that arose from it, written by a very talented young poet named Tim Giles:

uninhabited wind

The planet breathes.
Inhales, then gone.
It breathes.
There is nothing
but the hum of it.
Within vacant terrain.
The deep breath
passes through leaves
of bare trees.

Impossible to fathom
a single image
of the phantom.
Stop the breath
to let
the sunset be serene.

I especially love the first twelve lines of Tim's poem. I can almost feel the silence pressing in as the wind rustles through the barren branches of the oaks and the sycamores that stand near the creek edging the campus prairie, the stems of asters and goldenrod in the prairie itself, and the curled-up fists of Queen Anne's Lace blossoms among the lonely rattle of crinkly burdock leaves. I told Tim that his poem is like a

Tomas Transtromer poem meeting Wallace Stevens's snow man. Lovely.

Here's the assignment that inspired Tim's poem. Whether you're a teacher, a writer, or both, feel free to riff on this assignment in any way you like in order to make it more useful to you.

Thanks for listening.

S.D. Lishan

The purpose of this exercise is to help you pay attention, to focus on your attentiveness, to use another sense other than sight, to learn to rely on your journal, and to find some pearls among those icicles out there.

Now to the writing:

1. Go outside with your journal and something to write with.
2. If you're with someone, spread out. Find someplace where you can be alone for a while.
3. Be quiet.
4. As Tomas Transtromer advises in his poem "Midwinter," close your eyes.
5. Listen.
6. Write down what you hear.
7. Possible beginnings:
    i. I hear...
    ii. I close my eyes...
    iii. Or, like some of the examples above, you may want to start out by looking first and describe what you see ("Sunlight falls like cash through the canopy," "A blue light/ radiates from my clothing"). Don't be afraid to use figurative language (those things like metaphors and similes).

And like Mark Svenvold, with his "whistle and hoot," his "chitter" and "honk," his "bell and echo," and "whoopee cushion," try to use active verbs to describe what you're hearing. Be specific.

8. I'll remind you again. Be specific. Don't say something

uselessly general like, "I hear the glories of winter," or something similarly gloppy. Get down, dirty, and dangerous in your listening.

9. At some point—you'll know when—open your eyes and look with the same attention you brought to your listening. Feel free to touch, too. As Elizabeth Bishop says, *"Write it!"*

10. These will be rough lines, for, as Diane Thiel writes in her book about writing poetry, *Open Roads*, "journal entries are far from final pieces" (7). But it will be a start. When you're done, come back inside, rearrange, perhaps cut, perhaps change, and go from there, hopefully warmer in the knowledge that you've written some terrific lines. Enjoy.

Works Cited

Bishop, Elizabeth. "One Art." *Poetry Foundation*. n.d. Web. 23 July 2014.

Frost, Robert. "Stopping by Woods on a Snowy Evening." *Poetry Foundation*. n.d. Web. 20 Nov. 2013.

Giles, Tim. "uninhabited wind." Message to Stuart Lishan. 25 Nov. 2013. E-mail Hirschfield, Jane. "Section 26 of 'Song of Myself' and Whitman's Listening." *The Virginia Quarterly Review Spring* 2005: 48-49. Print.

Stevens, Wallace. "The Snow Man. *The Collected Poems of Wallace Stevens*. New York: Alfred A. Knopf, 1976. 9-10. Print.

Svenvold, Mark. "Ceiba Tree, Petac, Mexico." *The New Yorker*. 14 Nov. 2011, 34. Print.

Thiel, Diane. *Open Roads (Exercises in Writing Poetry)*. New York: Longman, 2004. Print.

Transtromer, Tomas, "Midwinter." *The Sorrow Gondola*. Trans. Michael McGriff & Mikaela Grassl. Los Angeles: Green Integer, 2010. 69. Print.

Whitman, Walt. "Song of Myself, Section 26." *Walt Whitman (Complete Poetry and Collected Prose)*. New York: The Library of America. 214-215. Print.

In Ink: Tattoo Images and Phrases

Janine Harrison

Target Audience: Beginner-to-intermediate level creative nonfiction writers
Purpose: Generate ideas for substantive short or long-form creative non-fiction texts

Exercise

According to Cate Lineberry in her article "Tattoos: The Ancient and Mysterious History," "Humans have marked their bodies with tattoos for thousands of years. These permanent designs—sometimes plain, sometimes elaborate, always personal—have served as amulets, status symbols, declarations of love, signs of religious beliefs, adornments and even forms of punishment" (1). For this exercise:

1. Please jot down a list of ten life-changing events. The events may be small ones and either positive or negative. Try to avoid major life occurrences that people often have and write about, such as driver's licenses, graduations, weddings, and babies.

2. Review your list and circle the three life events that most resonate with you—the ones in which you feel the pull of story.

3. Imagine that you are getting one tattoo for each of the three moments. What would each tattoo look like? Would it be an image or a phrase? What colors would be included? What size would it be? What purpose would the design serve? How would it symbolize your experience? Where would it be placed on your body? Would placement also be representative? If so, how?

4. Please free write for approximately ten minutes.

5. Now review what you have written. Which tattoo, which experience, do you most *want* to give voice? Which story *needs* to be given voice? Why? Explore this one further.

Works Cited

Lineberry, Cate. "Tattoos: The Ancient and Mysterious History."
    Smithsonian. (2007): 1. Web. 26 July 2014.

First Person Perspective Flash Fiction Prompts

Alexander Carrigan

A while back, I was writing a scene as part of an online collaborative role-playing game called *Survival of the Fittest*. The game, inspired by the 1999 Japanese Novel *Battle Royale* by Koshun Takami, was all about writing characters who find themselves forced to fight to the death on a deserted island. People playing this game had to create average high school aged characters and then write how they would handle the game, moving from scene to scene, bouncing off other characters and writers until certain prescribed events occurred. In one particular scene, I was playing a character named Claire, an eccentric, seventeen-year-old wannabe filmmaker from Seattle. I was writing a scene with Claire and another writer's character named Hansel, who at this point in the game was one of the more notable villainous characters. In the scene, Hansel was pointing a gun at Claire and taking her hostage following an action scene that resulted in the death of another character. Before Hansel's writer and myself could even get to this scene, there were a lot of steps we had to take to reach this moment.

First, we had to decide that this kind of scene was going to happen. Hansel had just killed an ally of Claire, and now he was threatening her, a decision that we agreed to once the game's rules declared that Claire's ally had to be written out of the story. Both Hansel's writer and I had been writing these characters for a few months before we reached this scene. I had spent the first few months of the game having Claire wander the island burying corpses and making pop culture references, while Hansel's writer had him go around and engage in deadlier scenes. We worked with other writers on the site to develop our characters by writing scenes that featured similar conflicts, all while keeping in mind that the game's rolling system could reveal that our characters would have to die as part of the overall narrative at any moment. These scenes helped shape the characters in the story and would lead to the moment the two crossed paths.

Before we even got to the game itself, we had to figure out exactly who the characters we were writing were as people. The premise of the game was that a group of seniors from a high school in Seattle were abducted by a terrorist group and trapped on a deserted island to fight to the death until one student remained out of 152 abducted students, but most writers on the site, including myself, had spent over a year preparing the characters for the game by detailing every aspect about the people we were writing. The game had guidelines for how we had to write the characters, but left room for us to develop them further.

For Claire, I had to think of everything about this person before I could write a single sentence of her story. I had to think about Claire's physical appearance, what her hobbies and interests were, what her personal history was, and what kind of people she'd call her friends. Beyond that, I had to think about how I, a male writer in his early twenties, would write a female teenage character, something I wanted to do but wasn't entirely comfortable with at the time. Going all the way back to the character's most basic attributes would allow me to completely understand who the character was and how she would handle the situations the game threw at her. While the character had a few missteps along the way, by the time I finished Claire's arc (sadly, she didn't survive the game), I felt like I truly understood who this person was, what her story was, and why she did the things she did in this extreme situation.

It was also around the point I discovered the game's website that I started to attend flash fiction events at my university. These events were hosted by school literary journals and required the writer to write short poems or prose pieces based on a chosen subject in a short period of time. Depending on the organization, this could mean that the attendees had to write about subjects ranging from "addiction" to "cat calling."

When I was at these events, I found that the easiest way for me to approach these subjects was to take what I used for *Survival of the Fittest*. I used the prompts and short time limit to write pieces that were written from the perspective of someone tied to the subject. At one such event, I won first place because I took a subject like "body modification" and wrote a piece in which a person imagines plastic surgery as being like the dress making scene from Disney's *Cinderella*. Doing so allowed me to develop a character and personality so that when I wrote about the morbid subject, I could convey a sense of being behind the piece.

It was because of all of this writing that I got to thinking how important it is to write first person pieces. I found that if you really try to develop a voice with your character, you can find something really worth writing. Developing a strong voice can create characters that can fit into a larger story. As someone who is very much interested in doing character-based writing, I find that trying to write short pieces from the perspective of an individual different from myself can yield worthwhile results. I'm able to disassociate myself from the character and think in entirely new ways. However, I'm also able to find a way to make this person who can be radically different from my own self still carry parts of my personality through the writing.

Because of this, I've developed a few flash fiction prompts that all have a leaning towards writing from the perspective of someone other than yourself. Use these exercises as a chance to play around with perspective, character, and tone. Try to go beyond your own personal opinion or way of thinking and try to create one for someone entirely different from yourself. Even if you don't write a story in the first-person perspective, doing these prompts can help you better understand a character and his/her motivation, which can hopefully help when you try to write a character for a larger story.

Below are fifteen flash fiction prompts to get started on this exercise. Each prompt has some additional questions to consider for the story you are writing, so feel free to take them into consideration when writing the piece. For each prompt, try to aim for about 300 words maximum. If you like what you're writing and are feeling a real connection with the piece, go beyond the word limit. If you feel you can take the prompt in an alternative direction, play around with it. The idea is to use these exercises as the starting point to create a character and maybe develop him/her further in another project of yours.

Prompts

1. Write a piece from the perspective of someone who is having the worst day ever. What's made it so bad? Is there anything that can make it better? Is this affecting their general outlook on life?

2. Write a piece about someone of the opposite gender doing something non-traditional. Are you a man doing something typically feminine? Are you a woman doing something typically masculine? What is driving you to do this activity? How do you feel doing this? Is there anything that might stand in the way of you doing this task?

3. Write a piece as if you are going on a long journey that you do not want to go on. Where are you going? Why are you going on this trip? What's so bad about this trip?

4. Write a piece from the perspective of someone who has just suffered an injury. What kind of injury is it? What's going through their mind as they lie in pain? Are there larger issues to come from this injury?

5. Write a piece from the perspective of someone who has lost something important. What is the thing they have lost? Why does it mean so much to them? Can they find it again, or is it gone forever?

6. Write a piece from the perspective of someone from a different social class than you and write about a simple task in their daily life. What challenges do they face? Are they similar or different from your own?

7. Write a piece from the perspective of someone in a hurry. Where are they going? What are they doing? What's keeping them from doing their task on time? What are the consequences of not completing this task on time?

8. Write a piece from the perspective of someone trashing the room they are in. Why would they trash this room? What is in the room to destroy? How do they go about destroying the room?

9. Write a piece from the perspective of someone in a different country than yours. How is their life different from yours? What are some challenges they face that you might not?

10. Write a piece from the perspective of someone half your age attempting to do something someone your age would normally do. Is it easy or difficult for this person to do? What challenges are they facing? Will they succeed or fail? If you'd like to try this prompt in another way, write from the perspective of someone twice your age attempting to do something someone your age would normally do. Does the fact that the character is older change the action? Is there something similar to how the young person and the old person do the chosen task?

11. Write a piece from the perspective of someone overhearing some characters trash talking them. Who are the characters that are talking? How venomous are their words? What does the viewpoint character think of what they are saying? Does the viewpoint character agree with what they're saying, or do they disagree? What is the next likely course of action for the viewpoint character?

12. Write a piece from the perspective of someone who is stuck in a room where two other people are having a nasty argument. What are those two fighting about? What does the viewpoint character think of the two arguing? Do they try to get the viewpoint character involved? Can the viewpoint character escape, or are they trapped in an awkward situation?

13. Write a piece from the perspective of someone who is teaching something they are knowledgeable about to someone who wants to learn from them. What kind of subject is being taught? Is the teacher confident in their abilities to teach, or are they doubting themselves? Is the pupil someone who will be easy to teach, or someone who will likely frustrate the teacher?

14. Write a piece from the perspective of someone who is coming home after being away for a long time. Are they coming home to anyone? Has anything about the person or their home changed since they have been away?

15. Write a piece from the perspective of someone who will suffer severe consequences if their encounter with another person goes horribly. Who are they meeting? What are the consequences of failing? What factors of this scenario will determine if the viewpoint character will succeed or fail?

Words as Inspiration
Kathleen Spivack

Introduction

I often work in countries where English is not the first language. Words, our ways of naming things, assume supreme importance. They carry intentionality: pebbles thrown out into a pond, the ripples spreading further. I have always liked to read dictionaries for pleasure, trying to memorize strange words and how to use them.

Writing in my first language, English, is no longer only the language of every day but something to be savored. I meet it on the page, a precious private tryst. It is my lover, with all the secrets and code-words that weave the fabric of our relation. *"Let me tell you how it is."* In intimacy, one briefly enters a borderland of gesture and murmured sounds. But at the truest moments of passion, whether in ecstasy or fury, our own words in our original language, the ones with the real power, those exact words that define what we are feeling, leap up and singe us.

The Exercise

This exercise is so simple: you just have to like reading and to have a pretty good dictionary. One might begin with an idea, a glimpse of something, an image, or a larger inclusive grouping of events about which to write. But it is not always easy to find the way in; there are so many possibilities. When working on a topic, any word, or collection of words, might be the starting point. It's like entering a labyrinth. Finding your way out is more difficult though. That's between you and the Minotaur.

1. Open an English Language Dictionary (if you are writing in English). I prefer the weight of an actual book on hand because it lends itself easily to random wandering and associations with a lazy turning of the pages. Reading a dictionary lures me the way the old libraries with their tottering card catalogues, their yellowing milky odor and open stacks used to do. They invite one to search further and deeper, each random word leading to another, touching the pages of books shelved

alphabetically until one day maybe you'd be found, locked in the underground maze of a great library, skeleton propped up at a little corral—books stacked high and a fresh one open before you. Writing is a bit like that, isn't it?

2. Now you're in front of the opened dictionary. Eyes closed, put your finger on a word: random page, random word. Then read about this word: origins, meaning, usage and so forth. Place the word on your tongue. Let it dissolve.

3. Write the word down at the top of a sparse white page. Your word is a bit of sun caught in a sunflower: it is petal and center, aura and corolla.

4. Let your mind wander outward from that word-center. Think of your project, what it is you intended to write about. Can this word be a touchstone, even if you don't actually use it? Enter its whole universe of meaning, the alpha and omega: memory and starting point.

Your word is a first step, a walk, an opening: it is your journey. If it is a long project, you might write down several words before starting, letting them resonate.

5. Now write two pages. Less. Or more. Usually by the end of the first paragraph I have an idea of the piece. Words become sentences, letting themselves be shaped. At the end of the writing time, I might write down a few key words to remind myself where I want to go the next day.

Many writing prompts include something like this. All it needs is one word to get the imagination going. Writers and teachers working with school children on their writing often use a "basket of words." The poetry magnets, so popular with refrigerators, also start with words, each one definite, stark, and associative. In France, where I have been teaching during the past few years, words are national treasures, to be cherished and protected.

If we have the words, with their many layers of meaning, we can witness and give voice. Living outside my own language has helped me appreciate the sensibility and structure of English as well as those of other languages. It has made me listen carefully to words and their meanings, their flaws, absences, and failures. There are words and there are also concepts for which individual languages have no words. That subtle area, which dictionary and thesaurus try to map, longs for exploration.

6. But by now we have digressed, and your writing still waits for you. Open the dictionary again. Touch another word. Listen to its sound. Let it whisper its secrets, its past, and what it has to say to you right now.

Twelve Workshops and a Void
Kazim Ali

Workshop Out Loud (Marie Ponsot)

Each student only brings one copy of their poem. Student reads the poem, and other students only listen. They may not take notes. Student reads the poem a second time or has the option to ask another student to read it. Students are not permitted to take notes this time either. Second reading is followed by no less than ten minutes of free-writing in response to the poem. As Marie Ponsot points out, entire books have been written on single haiku, so you should be able to manage ten minutes of writing on a poem. Discussion follows. Generally speaking, using this method, about three students, perhaps four, will be able to be workshopped during a three-hour once a week workshop. Recommended to cap the workshop at twelve students; each student receives a workshop at least three times during the average semester.

Workshop in the Dark (Jan Trumbauer)

All students lie in a circle, only their heads touching. Instructor covers all students with as large enough a sheet as is necessary. Instructor turns the lights off and maintains silence. Students take turns reciting their poems in dark. They must recite from memory since no writing can be seen. Other students respond and critique as normal. Students must speak in soft tones so that the instructor does not know what they are saying. Instructor's role is time-keeping and minimizing external disturbance or disruption only.

Workshop in Silence (John Cage)

Each student brings a poem to the workshop. Workshop begins with a five minute meditation. After this period, the poems are passed without discussion or comment. Poems are ordered by a pre-arranged agreement (so no verbal or somatic discussion is necessary). Using a bell or other timer, the poems are read silently. After the stack of poems are read quietly but together, the poems are discussed using hand gestures and facial expressions only. Students may indicate lines in the poem but all comments must be non-verbal. Students may optionally use interpretive dance or movement to give comments but no student may use any widely recognized non-verbal hand signals (such as an "OK" sign or "thumbs up" or actual ASL or other sign language).

Workshop in Yoga (Olga Broumas)

The first half of each workshop begins with a set of asanas associated with a particular energy chakra, beginning with the root chakra and proceeding up the spine through the sacral chakra, the abdominal chakra, heart chakra, throat chakra, third eye chakra, and sky chakra. Poems will be assigned the preceding week associated with this chakra. Poems are read and discussed after the asanas are completed. The second half of the workshop will be the set of asanas and poem assignment for the following week.

Agha Shahid Ali Workshop (Agha Shahid Ali)

This workshop will use Ali's *The Veiled Suite* in place of any other anthology or craft book. All lessons—prosody, poetic forms, personification, metaphor and metonym, etc.—will be drawn solely from exemplar poems from *The Veiled Suite*. At the culmination of the semester the students will mount a conference devoted to Ali's work at which they will present papers, host guest speakers, and conduct a group reading of Shahid's work which will include a program of poems they curate. Shahid's brother, sister, and father will be invited to this event.

Swarm Workshop (Jorie Graham)

This workshop will use as its starting point the volume *Swarm* by Jorie Graham. Other readings will include texts mentioned by Graham in connection with this work, including Thomas Traherne, Emily Dickinson, *Agamemnon*, *King Lear* and the following books of contemporary poetry: *Anathema* by David Jones, *Arcady* and *There Are Three* by Donald Revell, *Notes for Echo Lake* by Michael Palmer, *Pierce-Arrow* by Susan Howe, *Eros the Bittersweet* by Anne Carson, and *Sappho is Burning* by Page DuBois.

Workshop in Translation (Erin Moure)

All poems must be translated from another language even when (especially when) the student does not have working knowledge of that language. Homophonic and fake translations are also encouraged. If the student has invented a poet, they optionally also invent the language and the culture. In any case, biographical information, social and political context as well as some literary analysis of the poet's place in the canon of their own literature as well as discussion of particular difficulties of translating the invented poet are all required.

Collaboration Workshop (T Begley)

Eleven pieces to be discussed will be collaborations between two or more poets. Readings will be from poetic collaborations, including those by T Begley and Olga Broumas, David Trinidad and D.A. Powell, Dan Beachy-Quick and Srikanth Reddy, and Nikki Giovanni and Margaret Walker.

Workshop in Absentia (Bill Knott)

Students submit poems for workshop every week. Students meet in two halves. Students are not present for the workshop of their own poem. No student from the workshop may divulge to the poet anything about the discussion of that student's poem in the other group. Three times during the semester the full group will meet and the students will talk with the other half of the group about their poetry but will not refer to specific texts or lines.

Walking Workshop (Leslie Scalapino)

Variation of "Workshop Out Loud." This workshop, including the reading of the student poems and discussion, takes place completely while walking, preferably outside, preferably in a busy public setting.

Free-write portion does not take place. No note-taking or recording of discussion is permitted.

Workshop in Professional Practices (Etheridge Knight)

Each week the students engage in a different professional practice with their assigned poems. These include publishing a chapbook, editing a themed anthology, giving a planned public reading, performing guerilla public readings in (generally) non-literary spaces (shopping malls, parking garages, fast food restaurants, subway stations), placing signs or cards with poetry around in public places or hidden in libraries, written on chalkboards or on the sky.

Generative Workshop (Anne Waldman)

Rather than do critique/workshop, the class time is set aside for generating creative work. One can start with the exercises Anne Waldman sets out in *A Vow to Poetry*, but there are also many good exercises by Bernadette Mayer and those that appear in *The Practice of Poetry* by Robin Behn and Chase Twichell.

A Void: Workshop to Take Place in Your Mind (Yoko Ono)

The workshop does not meet. Every week at workshop time, students will sit at an empty table with their own poem and re-reread, revise, critique. All readings and writing assignments must be completed by appointed times. The instructor will go to the classroom assigned by the university every week and sit at the empty table for the entire duration of the class period. No attendance will be kept. No grades will be given.

218

Acknowledgements

We are grateful to all of the people who have helped make CREDO possible. A warm thanks to our wonderful assistant editors Alexander Carrigan and Megan Jeanine Tilley. For your meticulous attention, thank you to our copy-editors Emily Smith and Amanda R. Toronto. For your valuable advice on our book proposal, thank you to John Kulka from Harvard University Press. For your guidance and support, many thanks to Kathleen Spivack, David Shields, and Nell Irvin Painter. Thank you to the Cambridge Writers' Workshop board members and staff who have supported this project, including current interns Rachel Kurasz, Shannon O. Sawyer, and Anna-Celestrya Carr. To all of our contributing authors, thank you for being a part of CREDO and making your voices heard. To our literary agent Natalie Kimber at The Rights Factory, many thanks for your amazing support and representation. Finally, a huge thanks to our publishers at C&R Press, John Gosslee and Andrew Sullivan, who believed in the book and put in so much time and effort to share it with the world. Thanks to artist Eugenia Loli for the beautiful cover illustration, and thanks to all of the editors, readers, and designers at C&R Press. Thank you to the members and community of the Cambridge Writers' Workshop, to our literary partners, and to our friends and family for your inspiration, encouragement, and support.

Contributors

Kazim Ali's books include five volumes of poetry, *The Far Mosque, The Fortieth Day, Bright Felon, Sky Ward*, the winner of the Ohio Book Award for Poetry in 2014, and *All One's Blue: New and Selected Poems;* three novels, *Quinn's Passage, The Disappearance of Seth* and *Wind Instrument;* and three collections of essays, *Orange Alert: Essays on Poetry, Art and the Architecture of Silence, Fasting for Ramadan* and *Resident Alien: On Border-crossing and the Undocumented Divine.* He has translated books by Sohrab Sepehri, Ananda Devi and Marguerite Duras. He is an associate professor of Comparative Literature and the director of the Creative Writing Program at Oberlin College as well as the founding editor of the small press Nightboat Books.

Forrest Anderson's stories have appeared in *Blackbird, The Louisville Review, The South Carolina Review, The North Carolina Literary Review,* and elsewhere. A graduate of the doctoral creative writing program at Florida State University, where he worked for two years as an archivist and assistant for Robert Olen Butler, he also holds a Master of Fine Arts from the University of South Carolina. He lives in Salisbury, NC and is an associate professor of English at Catawba College.

Rita Banerjee is the author of *Echo in Four Beats* (Finishing Line Press, February 2018), the novella "A Night with Kali" in *Approaching Footsteps* (Spider Road Press, 2016), and the chapbook *Cracklers at Night* (Finishing Line Press, 2010). She received her doctorate in Comparative Literature from Harvard and her MFA from the University of Washington. Her writing appears in the *Academy of American Poets, Poets & Writers, Nat. Brut., The Scofield, The Rumpus, Painted Bride Quarterly, Mass Poetry, Hyphen Magazine, Los Angeles Review of Books, Electric Literature, VIDA: Women in Literary Arts,* and elsewhere. She is the judge for the 2017 Minerva Rising "Dare to Speak" Poetry Chapbook Contest, and is currently working on a novel, a documentary film about race and intimacy in the United States and in France, and a collection of essays on race, sex, politics, and everything cool. She is the founding Executive Creative Director of the Cambridge Writers' Workshop, and teaches at Ludwig-Maximilian University of Munich in Germany.

Lisa Marie Basile is the author of *APOCRYPHAL* and the chapbooks *Andalucia* and *war/lock*. She is the editor-in-chief of *Luna Luna Magazine*, and her poetry and essays have appeared in *PANK, Tin House, Coldfront, The Nervous Breakdown, The Huffington Post, Best American Poetry, PEN American Center, Dusie, The Ampersand Review*, and other publications. She's been featured in the *NY Daily News, Amy Poehler's Smart Girls* and on Ravishly.com. She holds an MFA from The New School and is working on a poetic novella.

Jaswinder Bolina is author of the poetry collections *The 44th of July* (2019), *Phantom Camera* (2012) and *Carrier Wave* (2006) and the chapbook *The Tallest Building in America* (2014). His poems have appeared widely in literary journals and in *The Best American Poetry* series. His essays have appeared at *The Poetry Foundation dot org, The Huffington Post, The Writer*, and in several anthologies including the 14th edition of *The Norton Reader*. Bolina is currently on faculty in the MFA Program at the University of Miami.

Stephanie Burt is a poet, literary critic, and professor. In 2012, the New York Times called Burt "one of the most influential poetry critics of her generation." She grew up around Washington, DC and earned a BA from Harvard and PhD from Yale. Burt has published three collections of poems: *Belmont* (2013), *Parallel Play* (2006), and *Popular Music* (1999). Burt's works of criticism include *Close Calls with Nonsense: Reading New Poetry* (2009), which was a finalist for the National Book Critics Circle Award; *The Art of the Sonnet*—written with David Mikics (2010); *The Forms of Youth: 20th-Century Poetry and Adolescence* (2007); *Randall Jarrell on W.H. Auden* (2005), with Hannah Brooks-Motl; and *Randall Jarrell and His Age* (2002).

Alexander Carrigan is the Communications and PR manager for the Cambridge Writers' Workshop and has been with the organization since 2014. He is currently a news copy editor for Rare.us. He has had fiction, poetry, reviews (film, TV, and literature), and nonfiction work published in *Poictesme Literary Journal, Amendment Literary Journal, Quail Bell Magazine, Luna Luna Magazine, Rebels: Comic Anthology* at VCU, *Realms YA Literary Magazine, Life in 10 Minutes,* and *Mercurial Stories.* He lives in Alexandria, VA.

Sam Cha received his MFA from UMass Boston. His work has appeared in *apt, Anderbo, Better, decomP, DIAGRAM, Cleaver, Printer's Devil Review, Memorious, Missouri Review, Rattle, RHINO,* and *Toad.* He's a poetry editor at *Radius* and at *Off the Coast.* He lives and writes in Cambridge, MA.

Melinda J. Combs' nonfiction work has appeared in *Women's Best Friend: Women Writers on the Dogs in Their Lives* and *Far From Home: Father-Daughter Travel Anthology.* Her fiction has appeared in *Gargoyle, Fiction Southeast* and *A Cappella Zoo.* She also teaches at Orange County School of the Arts in Santa Ana, California, where she listens to her students argue about the merits of magical realism in between their doodling and sighing.

Thade Correa hails from Northwest Indiana. He received his B.A. from Indiana University, his M.A. from the University of Chicago, and his M.F.A. from the University of Notre Dame. His poetry, translations, and essays have appeared in various venues. Recently, a collection of his work garnered him an Academy of American Poets Prize. A composer and pianist as well as a writer, he currently publishes his music with Alliance Publications. He works as a teacher of both writing and music.

Jeff Fearnside is author of the short-story collection *Making Love While Levitating Three Feet in the Air* (Stephen F. Austin State University Press). His writing has appeared in many literary journals and anthologies, including *Story, Rosebud,* and *The Pinch* (fiction); *The Fourth River, Permafrost,* and *The Los Angeles Review* (poetry); and *New Madrid, Potomac Review*, and *The Chalk Circle: Intercultural Prizewinning Essays*(nonfiction). Recipient of a 2015 Individual Artist Fellowship award from the Oregon Arts Commission, he teaches at Oregon State University and is at work on a novel. More info: www.Jeff-Fearnside.com.

Ariel Francisco is the author of *All My Heroes Are Broke* (C&R Press, 2017) and *Before Snowfall, After Rain* (Glass Poetry Press, 2016). Born in the Bronx to Dominican and Guatemalan parents, he completed his MFA at Florida International University in Miami. His poems have appeared or are forthcoming in *The Academy of American Poets, The American Poetry Review, Best New Poets 2016, Gulf Coast, Washington Square*, and elsewhere. He lives and teaches in South Florida.

John Guzlowski's writing appears in Garrison Keillor's *Writer's Almanac, Ontario Review, North American Review, Salon, Rattle, Atticus Review*, and many other print and online journals here and abroad. His poems and personal essays about his parents' experiences as slave laborers in Nazi Germany appear in his book *Echoes of Tattered Tongues* (Aquila Polonica Press, 2016). Of Guzlowski's writing, Nobel Laureate Czeslaw Milosz said, "He has an astonishing ability for grasping reality." Guzlowski's new novel *Road of Bones*. about two German lovers separated by war, is forthcoming from Kasva Press.

Rachael Hanel is a writer and assistant professor of mass media in Mankato, Minnesota, where she teaches an introductory mass media course and multimedia writing. Her memoir, *We'll Be the Last Ones to Let You Down: Memoir of a Gravedigger's Daughter* (2013, University of Minnesota Press), was a finalist for a Minnesota Book Award. She has written several nonfiction books for children. Her essays have appeared in online and print literary journals such as *Bellingham Review* and *New Delta Review*. She earned her Ph.D. in creative writing at Bath Spa University.

Janine Harrison, M.A., M.F.A., poet, nonfictionist, and fiction writer, teaches creative writing at Purdue University Calumet and leads the non-profit organization, Indiana Writers' Consortium. Her work has been published in *A&U; Veils, Halos, and Shackles* (Kasva Press) and other publications. She is currently finishing her first poetry collection, *The Weight of Silence*. Janine lives with her husband, fiction writer Michael Poore, and daughter, Jianna, in NW Indiana.

Lindsay Illich is an Associate Professor of English at Curry College in Milton, MA. Her work has appeared or is forthcoming in *Adirondack Review, Arcadia, Gulf Coast, Hunger Mountain, North American Review, Salamander*, and *Sundog Lit. Heteroglossia*, a chapbook, was published by Anchor and Plume in 2016. Her Twitter handle is @LindsayPenelope.

Douglas Charles Jackson lives and writes in Roanoke, Virginia, where he's exploring the intersections between books and place through BOOK CITY Roanoke (bookcityroanoke.com). His stories have been acknowledged with the Tennessee Writers Alliance Short Fiction Award, the James Andrew Purdy Award for Fiction, and the Bay to Ocean Fiction Award. Professionally, Doug coaches rural communities in downtown revitalization strategies, and he reports that, just like when he was at the head of the table in a workshop setting, he learns far more from the individuals and teams he's working with than he ever passes on to them. He's a graduate of Duke, UC Irvine, and the creative writing program at Hollins University.

Caitlin Johnson holds a Master of Fine Arts in Creative Writing from Lesley University. She is the author of two chapbooks: *Miles* (St. Andrews College Press, 2008) and *Boomerang Girl* (Tiger's Eye Press, 2015). Her first full-length poetry collection, *Gods in the Wilderness* was published by Pink.Girl.Ink. Press.

Christine Johnson-Duell is the author of the poetry chapbook, *Italian Lessons* (Finishing Line Press, 2014). Her work has appeared in *Poet*

Lore, CALYX, The Floating Bridge Review, The Far Field, Alimentum, The Boston Globe, The Seattle Times, Drash, and *Parent Map.* She is a Hedgebrook alumna and holds an MFA in Creative Writing from the University of Washington. A New Englander by birth, Johnson-Duell now lives in Seattle with her family.

Jason Kapcala lives in northern West Virginia along the Monongahela River where he finds inspiration in the frozen industry of Appalachia. His fiction and nonfiction has appeared in a number of magazines and journals, and he is the author of *North to Lakeville,* a collection of short stories published by Urban Farmhouse Press. He is currently writing a novel about a rock band from central Pennsylvania. His website is www.jasonkapcala.com

Richard Kenney's most recent book, *The One-Strand River,* was published by Knopf in 2007. He teaches at the University of Washington in Seattle, and at the Friday Harbor Laboratories on San Juan Island. He lives with his family in Port Townsend.

Eva Langston received her MFA in 2009 from the University of New Orleans, and her work has been published in many journals and anthologies, including *Compose Journal,* where she later became the Features Editor. She once won third place in a *Playboy Magazine* fiction contest, and her fiction has been nominated for the Pushcart Prize. In 2015 she was a San Miguel Literary Sala Writer-in-Residence, and for the past two years she has been an instructor at The Writer's Center in Bethesda, Maryland. A former high school math teacher, she now writes novels for teens and tweens. She lives in the D.C. area with her physicist husband and their young daughter. Follow her on Twitter at @eva_langston, or visit her blog at www.evalangston.com.

John Laue, is a former teacher, counselor, editor of *Transfer* and Associate Editor of *San Francisco Review.* He has won awards for poetry and prose, beginning with The Ina Coolbrith Poetry Prize at The University of California, Berkeley. With six published books to his credit, he presently coordinates the reading series of *The Monterey Bay Poetry Consortium* and edits the online magazine *Monterey Poetry Review*. In addition to his writing he is a mental health activist and a member and former Co-Chair of the Santa Cruz County California Mental Health Board.

S.D. Lishan is an Associate Professor of English at The Ohio State University. His book of poetry, *Body Tapestries* (Dream Horse Press), was awarded the Orphic Prize in Poetry. His poetry, fiction, and creative non-fiction have appeared in numerous journals such as *Arts & Letters, Kenyon Review, New England Review, Phoebe, Measure, Boulevard, Bellingham Review, Barrow Street, Your Impossible Voice, Brevity,* and *Creative Nonfiction.*

Ellaraine Lockie is a widely published and awarded poet, nonfiction book author and essayist. Her thirteenth chapbook, *Tripping with the Top Down,* was recently released from FootHills Publishing and has been selected as one of Winning Writers' Favorite Books from 2017. Earlier collections have won the Encircle Publications Chapbook Contest, the Poetry Forum Press Chapbook Contest Prize, San Gabriel Valley Poetry Festival Chapbook Contest, the Aurorean Chapbook Choice Award and Best Individual Collection Award from *Purple Patch* magazine in England. Ellaraine teaches poetry workshops and serves as Poetry Editor for the lifestyles magazine, *Lilipoh.*

Amy MacLennan has been published in *Hayden's Ferry Review, River Styx, Linebreak, Cimarron Review, Painted Bride Quarterly, Folio,* and *Rattle.* Her chapbook, *The Fragile Day,* was released from Spire Press in the summer of 2011, and her chapbook, *Weathering,* was published by Uttered Chaos Press in early 2012. She has a poem in the anthology *Myrrh, Mothwing, Smoke* that was published by Tupelo Press in March 2013. Amy's first full-length collection, *The Body, A Tree,* was released from MoonPath Press in early 2016. She lives in Ashland, OR

Kevin McLellan is the author of *Ornitheology* (The Word Works, 2018), *Hemispheres* (Fact-Simile Editions, 2018), [*box*] (Letter [r] Press, 2016), *Tributary* (Barrow Street, 2015), and *Round Trip* (Seven Kitchens, 2010). He won the 2015 *Third Coast* Poetry Prize and Gival Press' 2016 Oscar Wilde Award, and his poems appear in numerous literary journals. Kevin lives in Cambridge, Massachusetts.

E. Ce Miller is a writer, reader, activist, feminist, and yoga instructor. Currently she writes about books for *Bustle* magazine, and has been a writing mentor for the PEN America Prison Writing Program and the Afghan Women's Writing Project. Her words have appeared in *Culture Trip, Midwestern Gothic, Sixfold Journal, The Sun Magazine,* and more.

Brenda Moguez writes the kind of stories she loves to read—fiction, starring quirky, passionate women who are challenged by the fickleness and the complexities of life. She's particularly drawn to exploring the effects of love on the heart of a woman. Her forte is stripping away the protective layers concealing their doubts and insecurities and exposing the soul of her beautifully flawed characters. She has aspirations for a fully staffed villa in Barcelona and funding aplenty for a room of her own. When she's not working on a story, she writes love letters to the universe, dead poets, and Mae West. Her second novel was released in January 2016. You can find her at http://www.brendamoguez.com where she explores passionate pursuits in all its forms.

Peter Mountford is the author of the novels *A Young Man's Guide to Late Capitalism* (winner of the 2012 Washington State Book Award in fiction), and The Dismal Science (a NYT editor's choice). His work has appeared in *The Paris Review, Granta, Missouri Review, The Atlantic, The Sun,* and elsewhere. He is currently on faculty at Sierra Nevada College's MFA program, and is the events curator at Hugo House, Seattle's writing center.

Nell Irvin Painter is the Edwards Professor of American History, Emerita, at Princeton University and author of several books including *Sojourner Truth, A Life, A Symbol, The History of White People,* and *Standing at Armageddon: The United States, 1877-1919.* In addition to a Ph.D. in history from Harvard University, she holds a BFA from Mason Gross School of the Arts and an MFA the Rhode Island School of Design, both in painting. Her art school memoir is entitled *Old in Art School: A Memoir of Starting Over.*

Robert Pinsky went to college at Rutgers, The State University of New Jersey, and went on to graduate work at Stanford, where he held a Stegner Fellowship. *His Selected Poems* (Farrar, Straus, & Giroux) was published in 2011 and his new book of poems is *At the Foundling Hospital* (Fall, 2016). His previous books of poetry include *Gulf Music* (2008), *Jersey Rain* (2000), *The Want Bone* (1990) and *The Figured Wheel: New and Collected Poems 1966-1996.* His translation *The Inferno of Dante* (1994) was a Book-of-the-Month-Club Editor's Choice, and received both the Los Angeles Times Book Prize and the Harold Morton Landon Translation Award. His prose books include *The Life of David* (2005), *The Situation of Poetry* (1976) and *The Sounds of Poetry* (1998). Among his awards and honors are the William Carlos Williams Prize, the Harold Washington Award from the City of Chicago, the Italian Premio Capri, the PEN-Volcker Award, the Korean Manhae Prize, and a Lifetime Achievement Award from the PEN American Center. Robert Pinsky founded The Favorite Poem Project, including the videos that can be seen at www.favoritepoem.org, while serving an unprecedented three terms as United States Poet Laureate.

Kara Provost has published two chapbooks, *Topless* (Main Street Rag, 2011) and *Nests* (Finishing Line Press, 2006), as well as six microchapbooks with the Origami Poems project (origamipoems.com). Her poems have appeared in the *Connecticut Review, Main Street Rag, The Newport Review, Ibbetson Street, The Aurorean,* and other journals, as well as in *The Loft Anthology: 2012 Poetry Awards* and *In Praise of Pedagogy: Poetry, Flash Fiction, and Essays on Composing,* edited by David Starkey and Wendy Bishop. She teaches writing at Curry College in addition to conducting creative writing workshops for elementary students through adults. Currently, she is working on a full-length poetry manuscript as well as a chapbook combining visual design with poems based on the letters of the alphabet. She now lives near Providence, RI with her husband and two daughters.

Camille Rankine is the daughter of Jamaican immigrants. Her first full-length collection of poetry, *Incorrect Merciful Impulses*, was published in 2016 by Copper Canyon Press. She is also the author of the chapbook *Slow Dance with Trip Wire*, selected by Cornelius Eady for the Poetry Society of America's 2010 New York Chapbook Fellowship. The recipient of a 2010 "Discovery"/Boston Review Poetry Prize, she was featured as an emerging poet in the April 2011 issue of *O, The Oprah Magazine* and as one of *Brooklyn Magazine's* top 100 cultural influencers of 2017. Her poetry has appeared in numerous journals, including *The Baffler, Boston Review, Denver Quarterly, Narrative, Octopus Magazine, A Public Space, The New York Times* and *Tin House*. She serves on the Executive Committee of *VIDA: Women in Literary Arts*, chairs the Board of Trustees of *The Poetry Project*, and co-chairs the *Brooklyn Book Festival* Poetry Committee. She lives in New York City.

Jessica Reidy is a Brooklyn-based writer and professor. Her poetry, fiction, and nonfiction have appeared in *Narrative Magazine* as "Short Story of the Week," *The Los Angeles Review, Prairie Schooner*, and other journals. She is the winner of the Penelope Nivens award for Creative nonfiction, and her work has been nominated for the Pushcart Prize and Best of the Net. She's an editor for *The VIDA Review* and a Kripalu-certified yoga instructor, offering yoga and creative writing workshops. She also works her Romani ("Gypsy") family trades, palm and tarot reading, body work, and dancing in the New York area.

Amy Rutten has been writing seriously for the past five years, augmenting a 20-year career in architecture. She works for the Community of Writers at Squaw Valley and runs a vacation rental in Nevada City, California. She has published several short pieces in small publications and newspapers, and is just completing her first novel.

Elisabeth Sharp McKetta is the author of the biography *Energy* (Univ. Texas Press, 2017) as well as several previous books, including a writing guide. Her poetry and prose have been published in over 50 literary journals around the United States, including *Mid-American Review, Raintown Review*, and *The Coachella Review*. She teaches writing for Harvard Extension School. www.elisabethsharpmcketta.com.

David Shields is the internationally bestselling author of twenty books, including *Reality Hunger* (named one of the best books of 2010 by more than thirty publications), *The Thing About Life Is That One Day You'll Be Dead (New York Times* bestseller*), Black Planet* (finalist for the National Book Critics Circle Award), and *Other People: Takes & Mistakes* (Knopf, 2017). James Franco's film of *I Think You're Totally Wrong: A Quarrel* was also released in 2017. *The Trouble With Men: Reflections on Sex, Love, Marriage, Porn, and Power* is forthcoming next year. The recipient of Guggenheim and NEA fellowships and senior contributing editor of *Conjunctions*, Shields has published essays and stories in the *New York Times Magazine, Harper's, Esquire, Yale Review, Salon, Slate, McSweeney's*, and *Believer*. His work has been translated into two dozen languages.

Lillian Ann Slugocki has created a body of work on women and sexuality for print and for the stage including: The Public Theater, HERE, Circle Rep, Labyrinth Theater, *National Public Radio*, and *WBAI*. Her work has been published by Seal Press, Cleis Press, Heinemann Press, Newtown Press, Spuyten Duyvil Press, and *Salon, Bloom/The Millions, Beatrice, HerKind/Vida, Deep Water Literary Journal, Dr. T.J. Eckleburg Review, Non-Binary Review*, and *The Nervous Breakdown*. Her novella, *How to Travel with Your Demons*, was published by Spuyten Duyvil Press in 2015.

Maya Sonenberg is the author of the story collections *Cartographies* (winner of the Drue Heinz Prize for Literature) and *Voices from the Blue Hotel*. *26 Abductions*, a chapbook of her prose and drawings was published in 2015 by The Cupboard, and her newest chapbook of prose and photographs, *After the Death of Shostakovich Père*, won the PANK [Chap] book contest and will appear in 2018. Other fiction and nonfiction have appeared in *Fairy Tale Review*, *Web Conjunctions*, *DIAGRAM*, *New Ohio Review*, *The Literarian*, *Lady Churchill's Rosebud Wristlet*, *Hotel Amerika*, and numerous other journals, both in print and online. Her writing has received grants from the Washington State Arts Commission and King County 4Culture. She teaches in the creative writing program at the University of Washington.

Kathleen Spivack's novel *Unspeakable Things* was released by Knopf in early 2016. Her previous book, the memoir *With Robert Lowell and His Circle: Sylvia Plath, Anne Sexton, Elizabeth Bishop, Stanley Kunitz and Others* was published by the University Press of New England in 2012. Her chapbook, *A History of Yearning*, won the Sows Ear International Poetry Chapbook Prize in 2010, and she recently received the Allen Ginsberg, Erika Mumford, and Paumanok awards for her poetry. Her book won the New England Book Festival and London Book Festival Prizes. Published in over 400 magazines and anthologies, Kathleen's work has been translated into French. She has held grants from the National Endowment for the Arts; Massachusetts Artists Foundation; Bunting Institute; Howard Foundation; Massachusetts Council for the Arts and Humanities; is a Discovery winner and has been at Yaddo, MacDowell, Ragdale, Karolyi, and the American Academy in Rome. In Boston and Paris she directs the Advanced Writing Workshop, an intensive training program for professional writers. She has taught at conferences in Paris, Aspen, Santa Fe, Burgundy, Skidmore, and on the high seas, (Holland American Line).

Laura Steadham Smith's work has appeared in the *Gettysburg Review*, *Beloit Fiction Journal*, *Post Road*, and other magazines. She is the recipient of the Hamlin Garland Fiction Award and an AWP Intro Journals Prize. She currently lives and writes in Louisiana.

Molly Sutton Kiefer is the author of the full-length lyric essay *Nestuary* (2014) as well as three chapbooks of poetry, including *Thimbleweed*. Her work has appeared in *Hayden's Ferry Review, The Rumpus, PANK, Fiddlehead Review, Women's Studies Review,* and *Harpur Palate,* among others. She is co-founding editor of *Tinderbox Poetry Journal* and publisher of Tinderbox Editions. More can be found at www.mollysuttonkiefer.com

Jade Sylvan, called a "risque queer icon" by the Boston Globe, is an award-winning author, poet, screenwriter, producer, and performing artist heavily rooted in the literary and performance community of Cambridge and Somerville, Massachusetts. Jade's most recent book, *Kissing Oscar Wilde* (Write Bloody 2013), a novelized memoir about the author's experience as a touring poet in Paris (sponsored by a travel grant from The Foundation of Contemporary Arts), received rave reviews, and was a finalist for the New England Book Award and the Bisexual Book Award. Jade is now working on a bunch of slutty science fiction.

Anca L. Szilágyi's debut novel is *Daughters of the Air*. Her writing has appeared or is forthcoming from *Los Angeles Review of Books, Electric Literature,* and *Lilith Magazine,* among other publications. She is the recipient of the inaugural Artist Trust/Gar LaSalle Storyteller Award, a Made at Hugo House fellowship, and awards from the Vermont Studio Center, 4Culture, the Seattle Office of Arts & Culture, and the Jack Straw Cultural Center. *The Stranger* hailed Anca as one of the "fresh new faces in Seattle fiction." Originally from Brooklyn, she currently lives in Seattle with her husband. Find her at ancawrites.com or on Twitter @ancawrites.

Diana Norma Szokolyai is author of *Parallel Sparrows* (honorable mention for Best Poetry Book, 2014 Paris Book Festival), *Roses in the Snow* (first runnerup, Best Poetry Book, 2009 DIY Book Festival), and a feminist rewriting of a classic fairytale for Brooklyn Art Library's The Fiction Project, entitled *Beneath the Surface: Blue Beard, Remixed*. Szokolyai's poetry and prose has been published in *MER VOX Quarterly, VIDA Review, Quail Bell Magazine,* The Boston Globe, *Luna Luna Magazine, Up the Stair-*

case Quarterly, and has been anthologized in *Other Countries: Contemporary Poets Rewiring History, Teachers as Writers* & elsewhere. She's founding Executive Artistic Director of Cambridge Writers' Workshop.

Marilyn L. Taylor, former Poet Laureate of the state of Wisconsin (2009 and 2010) and the city of Milwaukee (2004 and 2005), is the author of six poetry collections. Her award-winning poems and essays have appeared in many anthologies and journals, including *Poetry, The American Scholar, Able Muse, Measure*, and in the Random House anthology titled *Villanelles*. Marilyn also served for five years as Contributing Editor and regular poetry columnist for *The Writer* magazine. She recently moved from Milwaukee to Madison, Wisconsin, where she continues to write and teach.

Megan Jeanine Tilley lives semi-aquatically in Tampa, Florida and has a deep enduring love for space and folklore. She received her BA in Creative Writing and MA in Literature from Florida State, and is currently working on a clinical doctorate in Audiology at University of South Florida. She has had several poems and short fictions published in journals and anthologies such as *Fiction Vale, The Deep Dark Woods, Wiley Writers, The Rectangle, Bracken*, and *Quail Bell Magazine*. Outside of writing, Megan is an avid collector of ghost stories and biscuit recipes.

Suzanne Van Dam loves the green and the wild, and finds plenty of it in the place she calls home, Michigan's Upper Peninsula. She is a writer for Little Brothers—Friends of the Elderly, an organization committed to reducing loneliness and isolation among the elderly. She also teaches creative writing, environmental studies, and English as a second language. She has an MFA from the University of Southern Maine's Stonecoast Creative Writing Program and recently completed her first novel, *Camp Redemption*. She writes frequently about the environment on themes ranging from frogs to snowshoeing, and from climate change to the precarious fate of bats in the wake of a deadly fungus that is wreaking havoc on bat populations throughout North America. One of her favorite pastimes is tagging along with scientists in the field and interpreting their scientific knowledge and intellectual passion for a lay audience. Her work has appeared in numerous environmental newsletters, along with *Traverse Magazine, Further North, The U.P. Environment, Ceramics Monthly*, and *Running Times,* among other publications.

Nicole Walker is the author of two forthcoming books *Sustainability: A Love Story* and *Love in the Ruins: A Survival Guide for Life after Normal.* Her previous books include *Where the Tiny Things Are: Feathered Essays, Egg, Micrograms, Quench Your Thirst with Salt,* and *This Noisy Egg.* She also edited *Bending Genre* with Margot Singer. She's nonfiction editor at *Diagram* and Associate Professor at Northern Arizona University in Flagstaff, Arizona where it rains like the Pacific Northwest, but only in July.

Allyson Whipple is an MFA candidate at the University of Texas at El Paso. She is the author of two chapbooks, most recently *Come Into the World Like That* (Five Oaks Press, 2016). Allyson teaches business and technical communication at Austin Community College, and is working on her first full-length collection.

Shawn Wong is the author of two prize-winning novels, *Homebase* and *American Knees*, and editor/co-editor of six Asian American and American multicultural literary anthologies including the pioneering anthology *Aiiieeeee! An Anthology of Asian American Writers.* The film version of *American Knees*, titled "Americanese" won several film festival awards in 2006. Wong was featured in the Bill Moyers' PBS documentary, "Becoming American: The Chinese Experience," in 2003. He is currently Professor of English and Comparative Literature, Cinema and Media at the University of Washington.

Caroll Sun Yang earned her BFA at Art Center College of Design, an MFA in Creative Writing from Antioch University and holds certification as a Psychosocial Rehabilitation Specialist. Her work appears in *The Nervous Breakdown, New World Writing, The Los Angeles Review of Books, McSweeney's IT, Necessary Fiction, Word Riot, Columbia Journal, Diagram* and *Juked.* She is the Associate Editor for *The Unseasonal.* She survives in Highland

Park, Ca with her family of four and yearns for more personality-disordered friends/ lo-fi anything/ sarcasm/ art films featuring teens/ Latrinalia/ frosting flowers/ bio changes. She spews forth as Caroll Sun Yang on Facebook/ IG -- www.carollsunyang.com.

Matthew Zapruder is the author of four collections of poetry, most recently *Come On All You Ghosts*, a *New York Times* Notable Book of the Year, and *Sun Bear* (Copper Canyon 2014). *Why Poetry*, a book of prose, was published by Ecco Press in 2017. He has received a Guggenheim Fellowship, a William Carlos Williams Award, a May Sarton Award from the Academy of American Arts and Sciences, and a Lannan Foundation Residency Fellowship in Marfa, TX. An Associate Professor in the St. Mary's College of California MFA program and English Department, he is also Editor at Large at Wave Books. He lives in Oakland, CA.

OTHER C&R PRESS TITLES

NONFICTION

Women in the Literary Landscape by Doris Weatherford, et al

FICTION

Made by Mary by Laura Catherine Brown
Ivy vs. Dogg by Brian Leung
While You Were Gone by Sybil Baker
Cloud Diary by Steve Mitchell
Spectrum by Martin Ott
That Man in Our Lives by Xu Xi

SHORT FICTION

Notes From the Mother Tongue by An Tran
The Protester Has Been Released by Janet Sarbanes

ESSAY AND CREATIVE NONFICTION

Immigration Essays by Sybil Baker
Je suis l'autre: Essays and Interrogations
by Kristina Marie Darling
Death of Art by Chris Campanioni

POETRY

Dark Horse by Kristina Marie Darling
Lessons in Camouflage by Martin Ott
All My Heroes are Broke by Ariel Francisco
Holdfast by Christian Anton Gerard
Ex Domestica by E.G. Cunningham
Like Lesser Gods by Bruce McEver
Notes from the Negro Side of the Moon by Earl Braggs
Imagine Not Drowning by Kelli Allen
Notes to the Beloved by Michelle Bitting
Free Boat: Collected Lies and Love Poems by John Reed
Les Fauves by Barbara Crooker
Tall as You are Tall Between Them by Annie Christain
The Couple Who Fell to Earth by Michelle Bitting

CHAPBOOKS

Atypical Cells of Undetermined Significance by Brenna Womer
On Innacuracy by Joe Manning
Heredity and Other Inventions by Sharona Muir
Love Undefind by Jonathan Katz
Cunstruck by Kate Northrop
Ugly Love (Notes from the Negro Side Moon) by Earl Braggs
A Hunger Called Music: A Verse History in Black Music
by Meredith Nnoka

CPSIA information can be obtained
at www.ICGtesting.com
Printed in the USA
FSHW01n1538020518
47542FS

9 781936 196838